Salamis 480 BC

The "Wooden Walls" that saved Greece

Salamis 480 BC

The "Wooden Walls" that saved Greece

K. PAPADEMETRIOU - G. KOUFOGIORGOS - K. GRIGOROPOULOS - D. VARSAMI

AUTHORS
K. Papademetriou - G. Koufogiorgos
K. Grigoropoulos - D. Varsami

EDITORS (ENGLISH EDITION)
Nikos Giannopoulos, *Historian*
Stelios Demiras

TRANSLATOR
Thanos Mentzelopoulos

PROOF EDITOR
Charles Davis

COVER ART
Christos Giannopoulos

UNIFORM RESEARCH AND RECONSTRUCTION-ILLUSTRATION
Christos Giannopoulos

SHIP PROFILES
Dimitris Hadoulas

ART DIRECTOR AND COVER DESIGN
Dimitra Mitsou

MAPS
Georgia Karapati

PICTURE CREDITS
Authors' Archives, Periscopio Publications' Collection

First published in Greece in 2008
by Periscopio Publications
in cooperation with Squadron/Signal Publications

Distributed worldwide exclusively
by Squadron/Signal Publications
1115 Crowley Drive
Carrollton, TX 75006-1312 U.S.A.
www.SquadronSignalPublications.com

© 2008 Periscopio Publications

All rights reserved. Reproduction in part or in whole is forbidden without prior written permission from the publisher, except in case of brief quotations used in reviews.

ISBN: 978-0-89747-567-9

KONSTANTINOS PAPADEMETRIOU
Konstantinos Papademetriou was born in Athens. He is a graduate of the Law and Political Science Department of the University of Athens. He has a Master's degree in Public Law and Administrative Science, while now he is a PhD candidate on greek state institutions. As a graduate of the National School of Public Administration he is a civil servant and now serves in the independent authority "Citizen's Councelor." He has written many articles on ancient and modern Greek history.

KYRIAKOS GRIGOROPOULOS
Kyriakos Grigoropoulos was born in Athens in 1979. He studied history and archeology at the Philosophy Department of the University of Athens, graduating in 2001 with a degree in Archeology. He continued his studies at the same university and, during 2003, also studied at the University of Oxford under the ERASMUS program. Kyriakos attained his post-graduate degree in Prehistoric Archeology in 2004. At present, he is working on his doctorate degree at the University of Athens under a Greek state scholarship. As a pre- and post-graduate student, Kyriakos has participated in archeological excavations and research projects in Greece and Turkey. He has also published a number of articles on archeological and historical subjects. His primary interests include the relationships of wars, societies and ideologies, not only of the Aegean prehistoric period but also of the whole of the ancient world of the Mediterranean region.

GEORGE KOUFOGIORGOS
George Koufogiorgos was born in 1969. He is a graduate of the School of Philosophy of the University of Ioannina, Greece, with postgraduate studies in Medieval Studies at the same university, as well as in Italy under special scholarship. He works as a teacher of literature at a private school. As a valued contributor to "Periscopio Publications," he has contributed articles in "Military History" magazine and the "Great Battles" monographs, while he is also the author of the "Flames of War" series.

DESPOINA VARSAMI
Despoina Varsami was born in Athens and is a graduate of the Faculty of Philosophy, Pedagogics and Psychology of the School of Philosophy of the University of Athens. Ms Varsami works as a teacher. She has undertaken the writing and publishing of monographs, scientific articles and encyclopaedic entries of philological, pedagogical and historical content. Despoina is the author of the *Pericles and the Peak of the Athenian Democracy* monograph, published by Periscopio Publications in 2004, as well the book *Theory and Practice of Pedagogics* published by Kritiki in 2008).

CHRISTOS GIANNOPOULOS
Christos Giannopoulos, an illustrator and character designer, was born in 1968 in Athens. Although he has a degree and professional experience in Social Work, he has developed a special interest in ancient and medieval history. Christos has worked for 14 years as a professional artist and has produced illustrations for many children's titles, multimedia projects, and a number of books on ancient, medieval, and modern warfare. With his unlimited interest in figure design and uniform research, Christos has created original illustrations that have been a source of inspiration for a number of miniature sculptors producing figures for model companies, including Romeo Models and Pegaso Models of Italy, and Seil Models of Korea. His favored fields of study and research are Ancient Greek hoplite warfare, Celtic Europe, Central Asian cultures, and Roman Britain.

Contents

8 The naval Battle of Salamis
The decisive naval conflict that saved the fledgling European culture
by K. Papademetriou

46 The "Wooden Walls"
Themistocles' stratagem
by G. Koufogiorgos

48 The trireme
The warship of the two rival fleets during the naval Battle of Salamis
by K. Papademetriou

66 Themistocles
Victory's guide
by D. Varsami

78 The Persian point of view regarding the Battle of Salamis
by K. Grigoropoulos

88 "Themistocles' Trophy" and the "Salamis Warriors' tomb"
In search of the heroes' bones
by K. Grigoropoulos

92 Naval Battle memories
by K. Papademetriou

96 Bibliography

Preface

Following the triumph of the hoplites at Marathon and Thermopylae, it was the turn of the Greek oarsmen to take a stand at Salamis for everything the great Greek civilization had accomplished within the political framework of the city-state. The free, non-submissive Greek citizens, armed with resolution, moral fortitude, and agility of wit, not only confronted illiberal Persian despotism, but also the Greek moody idiosyncrasy that at times led to successes and victories while, at others, produced failure and disappointment. Themistocles, the tactical genius who decisively commanded the Greek forces, led Greece to victory and eternal glory. The great Athenian general, some of whose character traits were undecipherable even to his fellow citizens, became famous as the man who "sank the Persian dream." His decisions were critical, while his responsibilities towards his nation and European history were immense, if the reader takes into account the way he led, not only the Persians but also the Greeks, toward the chosen site of this naval battle.

Nikos Giannopoulos
Editor

The naval Battle of Salamis

The decisive naval conflict that saved the fledgling European culture

Thanks to the decisiveness of Themistocles and his inspired leadership, and to some 75,000 Greek seamen, the majority of whom were simple people, the Greek fleet managed to crush and repel an invasion from Asia. The heroic naval battle that took place in the waters of the Saronic Gulf near Athens, allowed not only Greece, but all of Europe to develop its human-oriented culture.

Yet as Peter Green, the American Professor of Classical Studies, has most cogently pointed out, the Battle of Salamis, "despite its momentous importance ... should be considered as one of the most badly argued battles in the whole history of sea warfare," (a note in the book *Greco-Persian Wars* published in English in 1996). The exceptional importance of the engagement, the many fables woven around its conduct, the contradictory accounts related by the ancient sources, the input of many subsequent writers with various levels and types of expertise (historians, historiographers, seamen, military men, engineers, scholars, and others), and the multitude of different assessments that have been expounded over the centuries, have all conspired to obscure the image of the event more than elucidate the facts. In modern times, Greek university professor Konstantinos Rados contributed greatly to clearing up the confusion when in 1915 he published his study reviewing and analyzing the contradictory accounts of the battle. Certain minor questions still remain, however, and it is this relative ambiguity coupled with the fundamental importance of the battle, that serve constantly to stimulate historians, seamen, shipbuilders, geologists, historical anthropologists, sociologists, political scientists, engineers, and others to undertake further research and thereby demonstrate that even after the passage of nearly 2,500 years, interest in the Battle of Salamis remains undiminished.

Sources for the battle

A first and basic source on the momentous conflict, as well as on all the operations during the Persian Wars, is the work of "the father of history," Herodotus, who wrote only a few decades after the battle. Aeschylus, one of Ancient Greece's most decorated poets and playwrights who apparently participated in the battle as a marine aboard an Athenian trireme, left us an exceptionally dramatized description in his play *The Persians,* mentioning many elements that, in general, tend to agree, confirm, or supplement Herodotus' narrative. Their differences are few and relatively unimportant, as for example in the numbers of boats. What Aeschylus wrote was a work of art and not a scientific historical study, but he cannot have made serious mistakes, given the fact that he himself participated in the battle, that he

The naval Battle of Salamis

"Triremes in Hot Pursuit." Painting by Christos Giannopoulos.

A sculptured monument at Behistun, where, by order of Darius, his victories over the usurpers were carved. Usurpers are depicted being tied by the neck, while Darius's figure dominates on the left.

wrote the tragedy soon afterwards, and that he presented it before an audience that had either direct experience or knew the facts of the event. Thucydides, who wrote a little later (at the close of the 5th Century BC), makes only limited references to the Persian Wars, and offers us just a little additional information. Also, from the very few existing texts of Ctesias, a Greek doctor in the court of the Persian king Artaxerxes II (early 4th Century BC), we can glean information on the Persian version and the estimations of the opposing side concerning the great conflict. We cannot, however, have complete confidence in Ctesias, on the one hand because he wrote while living under an authoritarian regime and, on the other hand because his book is full of exaggerations that clearly limit his reliability.

Much later, in two of his *Parallel Lives* (those of Themistocles and Aristeides), Plutarch preserved many details concerning the battle and illuminated various features of the personalities of the two Greek leaders. His narratives, written in the late 1st Century AD, agree, to a large extent, with Herodotus' descriptions, although Plutarch does not appear to have particularly appreciated him.

Ephorus, a 4th Century BC historian, took a different perspective from that of Herodotus, even though he used him as his basic source. The facts themselves are not in dispute, but their presentation is different and, as a rule, their interpretation also differs. Very few of Ephorus' texts have been preserved, but some of his work has survived because another important historian, Diodorus Siculus, made use of it in his multi-volume *Library of History*, written in the 1st Century BC. Diodorus sparked heated discussions and much disagreement, because he presented a version differing from that of Herodotus regarding the exact site of the crucial naval battle (at the opening of the narrows around Psyttaleia, in a north-to-south direction, and not inside the narrow area, in an east-to-west one). Certain useful points can also be obtained from the work of Isocrates, the poet Pindar, the philosophers Plato (*Menexenus*) and Aristotle (*The Constitution of the Athenians and Politics*), and from the leading composer of epigrams, Simonides of Kea.

The road to war

Following the collapse of the Greek defensive line at Thermopylae (end of August 480 BC) and the willing subjugation of almost all the Boeotian states (except Plataea and Thespiae which were, in consequence, destroyed by the Asian invaders), a large Persian army arrived in the northern area of Attica in September 480 BC.

The city of Athens, being under direct threat, faced an exceptionally difficult situation. The allied army was not only absent, but soon the decision to create a front at Isthmus would be announced, where the various Peloponnesian units had already begun to assemble and construct a defensive line. It was obvious that they

A depiction of the eastern portico of the Temple of Aphaea Athena at Aegina, showing battle scenes.

did not intend to advance to the east in order to prevent a Persian advance on Athens. In a state of widespread concern and fear, the leader of the democratic party and one of the ten generals, Themistocles, son of Neocles, who was apparently recognized as the Commander-in-Chief, rose to the occasion with remarkable energy. Following his directives, the Athenian Municipality decided to evacuate the city and transfer the entire population to the neighboring island of Salamis (which belonged to the state of Athens), to the island of Aegina, and to the hospitable region of Troezen, which had always maintained good relations with Attica (Theseus' place of origin). Simultaneously, the whole of the military preparations were focused on the naval force, especially on the 180 triremes that the city could array in battle.

According to a well-known prophecy of the Delphic oracle, "wooden walls" would save Athens. Some citizens considered these walls to be those that covered the entrance to the Acropolis and insisted on barricading themselves behind them and making their final stand there. Themistocles, however, with great determination, rejected this unrealistic interpretation of the prophecy and declared that the oracle referred solely to Athens' fleet of ships. Thus, the Athenians turned to the ships during those dramatic days of September 480 BC; on the one hand, all the civilians embarked for Salamis, Aegina, and Troezen while, on the other hand, all those fit for battle manned the warships and prepared for the expected confrontation. The relative descriptions are most vivid: over 200,000 people of all ages (including their slaves) abandoned their houses, their estates, and their forefathers' homes to become refugees, without knowing whether they would ever return. Only those too ill to move remained in the deserted city – together with a few hopeless romantics who believed in some divine intervention for salvation. These took cover on the Acropolis.

The Persians reached Athens shortly after the last ship departed from the port of Piraeus. Having arrayed their army towards Eleusis as well as Messogeia and Cape Sounion, they triumphantly entered the deserted city. They massacred the very few old and sick they found on the streets and in the houses and then laid siege to the Acropolis. Here, those few aristocratic Athenians who believed to the end that salvation would come from the intervention of the Spartans or of the gods defended themselves bravely and tenaciously. But, after a number of the Persians climbed the steep northern side of the Acropolis and attacked the handful of defenders from the rear, all resistance collapsed. The invaders put all the defenders to the sword and then, showing no respect for the sacred site, they set fire to everything, burning all the temples, the statues of gods, the oblations, even the holy olive tree of Pallas Athena. After plundering the rest of the city, the Persians subjected it to the same fate as the Acropolis, and the Persian

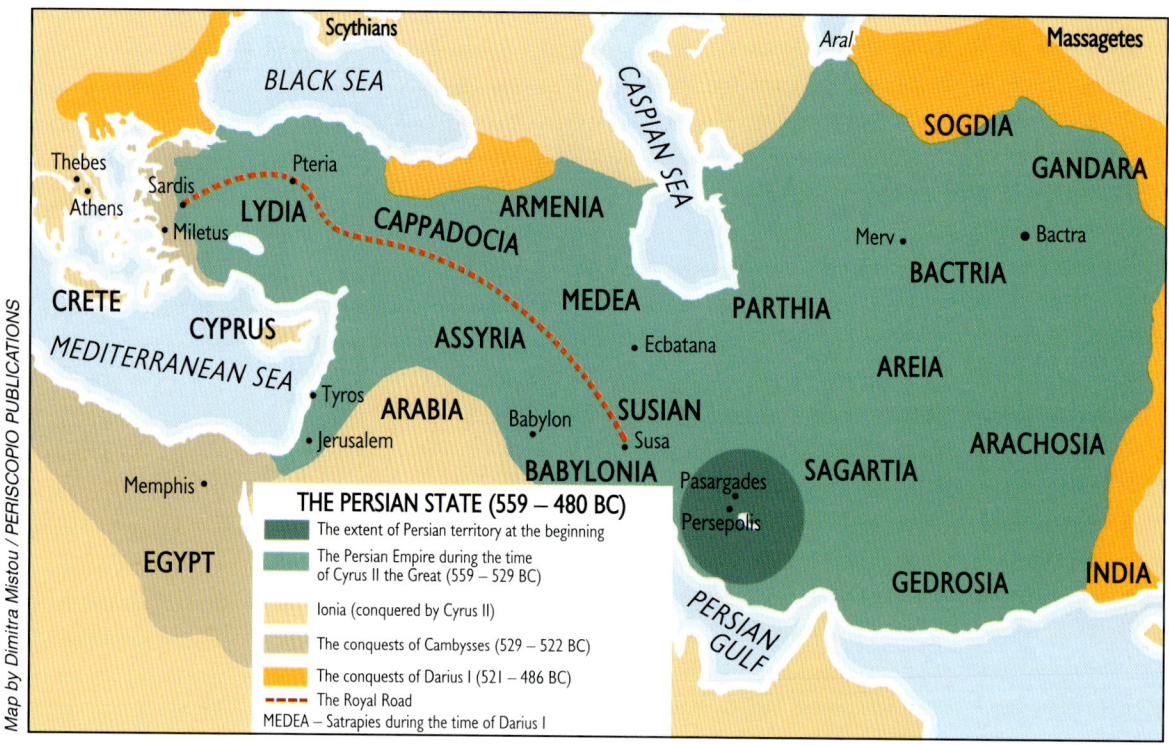

King Xerxes sent a messenger to his capital Susa, in what is today southwestern Iran, to convey the news of his success.

This victory was, however deceptive, since actual success in the conduct of war – its main strategic aim – is always to crush the opponent's forces and not to occupy his territory. It was even more deceptive, in fact, as the Persians' actual opponents were not far away. After their retreat from Artemisium, the Greeks had assembled at Salamis and set up a powerful naval camp. The front line was, henceforth, extended to the marine area between Attica and Salamis. The Persian naval force of 700 warships arrived and anchored in Phaleron Bay, this being close to and allowing contact with their ground forces.

Xerxes and his large entourage settled near the sea. There the king held council with his military commanders concerning their future strategy. For a few days the two protagonists kept their distance and weighed each other up. The Greeks were anchored along the Eastern coasts of Salamis, while the Persians were ranged along the western coast, from Piraeus to Phaleron, with neither side daring to take an active initiative.

The opposing forces

The strengths of the opposing naval forces are still not known with absolute precision. They can, however, be estimated based on some calculations.

The Greeks

Herodotus affords us detailed and reliable information as far as the Greek forces are concerned. Moreover, since his texts became widely known in the Greek world (they were recited during the great feasts in Athens and, possibly, other cities also), any incorrect recording would had been detected and

The naval Battle of Salamis 13

LACEDAEMONIAN CHIEFTAIN (489 – 479 BC)
This illustration depicts the classical image of an officer from southwestern Laconia. He wears a Corinthian helmet with the typical transverse Doric crest, a hoplite shield with the design of a bull's head (considered to be one of the eight emblems characterizing the Spartan morae), and an early version of the muscular cuirass and bronze greaves. It is highly unlikely that cuirasses or greaves were used by the Lacedaemonians, or other Greek epibatae (marines) during the naval Battle of Salamis. (Uniform research and reconstruction - illustration by Christos Giannopoulos)

discussed. Although the "father of history" writes about 378 triremes in total, in the detailed record of the ships that each state separately contributed to the Greek naval force during that September, he gives the following numbers (see table).

Altogether, therefore, there were about 368 and not 378 triremes. In addition, there were also 14 pentaconters. Consequently, the grand total amounted to 382 warships. Twelve more triremes, guarding the island of Aegina, should be added to the Greek fleet's total force, as well as a further 60 triremes from Corfu that had been arrayed off the Peloponnese west coast, but without any clear idea of their intentions. Adding the Corfiot ships results in a total of 394 warships, this being very close to the (possibly rounded-up) number of 400 Greek warships given by Thucydides. This figure, however, simply reveals the number of the Greek fleet's existing ships. The available vessels that actually participated in the naval engagement were 382, with the 368 triremes having the dominant role, supported by the 14 pentaconters that probably only provided auxiliary services.

This grand armada of ships was crewed by approximately 75,000 men, of whom 4,000 to 5,000 were marines (*epibatae*) and the rest 70,000 seamen (of whom 63,260 were rowers). In addition, the Athenian ships, and probably also others, each carried a detachment of archers (four on each Athenian trireme), giving a total of 800 to 1,000 bowmen.

The Persians

Calculating the size of the Persian forces is a much more difficult affair. Whereas the number of Xerxes' ships at the beginning of the expedition, as detailed by Herodotus as well as Diodorus Siculus, is not disputed (roughly 1,200 warships, of which another 120 were added by the coastal cities of Thrace and the islands of the northern Aegean: Samothrace, Thassos, Lemnos, etc.), the exact number of ships that finally deployed against the Greeks in the Strait of Salamis has been the subject of serious arguments among historians. These disagreements arose from the difficulties encountered by ancient historians, firstly by Herodotus himself, in precisely determining the losses suffered by the Persians through storms and from the naval operations around Cape Artemisium. According to Herodotus, the losses sustained by the Persian royal fleet off the coasts of Magnesia amounted to 400 triremes (obviously the number was rounded up). A further 45 ships fell into Greek hands during two different operations near the harbor of Aphetai, while in

Cites	*Triremes*
Athens	180
Corinth	40
Aegina	30
Megara	20
Chalkis	20
Sparta	16
Sicyon	15
Epidaurus	10
Ambracia	7
Eretria	7
Troezen	5
Naxos	4
Hermione	3
Leukas	3
Kea	2
Styra	2
Kythnos	1
Croton	1
Lemnos	1 (that defected after Artemisium)
Tenos or Tenedos	1 (that defected before the naval battle)

The naval Battle of Salamis

Coela of Euboea another 200 were lost to storms, including Cilicia's entire naval force (100 triremes). The total of these losses was 645 ships. To this number, however, should be added those vessels that were damaged beyond repair or sunk at the naval battle in Artemisium in August 480 BC, the number of which still remains unknown. The figure was not, in any case, overly impressive, otherwise the total or, at least, its influence on the course of the events would have been recorded. As it was not, then the actual number must have been relatively small. Finally, the Persians were deprived of the services of two triremes (one each from Lemnos and Tenos/Tenedos), which defected to the Greek naval force (where they obviously belonged). The certified losses of these 647 ships and the assumed loss of another 50 to 70 at Artemisium, makes a total of 700 to 720 warships that had been eliminated from Xerxes' force, leaving him with roughly 600 vessels.

This estimate is in agreement with two remarks, one by Herodotus and the other by Achaemenes, the Persian admiral. The Greek historian, in his narrative concerning the operations at Cape Artemisium, stated that, after the auspicious (to the Greeks) destruction of the 200 Persian ships that had tried to outflank them, the number of ships remaining to the Persians did not greatly exceed those of the Greeks. Similarly, the Persian admiral Achaemenes, commander of the Egyptian fleet, soon after the battle at Artemisium, reported to King Xerxes that the Persian fleet outnumbered the Greek fleet by 300 ships. Consequently, since the Persians were probably aware that the Greek fleet that was lined up in Artemisium consisted of just over 300 (324 precisely) ships, they determined their own fleet to consist of between 600 and 630 ships.

To the 600 to 630 Persian warships, a number that we have adopted, were added some reinforcements, although the number was never defined. Herodotus calculated that these reinforcements, which consisted of Greeks from the regions under Persian occupation (e.g. Karystos and Aulis), as well as of a number of islands (e.g. Andros, Tenos, Skopelos, Skiathos, Skyros, etc.), compensated for the already recorded losses. But what Herodotus himself records as an assumption cannot be valid. The Greek islands were unable to deploy such large naval forces at that time, regardless of their number. Knowing precisely the naval units of those islands that allied themselves with the Greeks, a safe conclusion can also be made concerning the islands that sided with the enemy. Athens' powerful ally Aegina could array 42 ships, Leukas just three, important Naxos only four, Kea one, Kythnos one, and so on. Given these data, it is beyond reasonable belief that the small island states of the northern and central Aegean could contribute 400 – 600 ships to the Royal Persian Fleet as implied by Herodotus and the historians who agree with him. Similarly, the Greeks of Locris, Boeotia, and Eastern Euboea could

The Temple of Aphaea Athena at Aegina. Built around 500 BC, it is indicative of the economic and social progress of the island at that time. Twenty years later, Aegina was able to offer 42 ships to the Greek allied fleet; 30 of them participated at the Battle of Salamis.

have possessed but very few ships (if indeed they had any). Their contribution to the Persian fleet would of necessity only be very limited, no matter how much pressure was placed on them. Counting, therefore, one to five ships for each one of approximately 20 small inlands and island states, gives a result of a reasonable 70 to 80 ships. These reinforcements raised the Persian fleet's total number to approximately 700 operational warships that sailed without interference and anchored in Phaleron Bay at the beginning of September 480 BC.

This estimate of approximately 700 ships is indirectly confirmed by discussions held by Xerxes' staff prior to the naval battle. During the evaluation of various proposals, the one that finally prevailed was to split the force into two squadrons, with one moving towards the Peloponnese and the other remaining on station in order to keep an eye on the Greeks in Salamis. But Admiral Achaemenes objected that, by doing so, the Persians would also lose their numerical advantage over the Greek naval force at Salamis. Considering that the Persians, either by direct observation (something relatively easy from the opposite coast) or by spies or Greek fugitives, had been informed about the size of the naval force opposing them (350 to 400 ships maximum), once again we may conclude that, at that time, they were able to array a number of ships almost double that of the Greek fleet. In this manner, the estimate of a total of 700 available Persian ships is substantiated.

The Persian Fleet carried approximately 150,000 to 155,000 men. This increased number was the result of an order by the Persian high command to add a further 30 to 40 warriors to each ship's complement.

This measure was probably adopted to enable the Persians to confront the Greek marines more effectively, even though, according to another version, it was a measure of the Persian commanders' lack of confidence in the disparate crews that constituted their multinational fleet.

General characteristics of the area

Attica is in the form of a right angle, with one side extending horizontally towards the northwest and the other extending to the south. Salamis is located inside this angle. It has a somewhat irregular shape, but generally follows Attica's coastline, shaping narrower channels (the passage of Megara – Nisaia in the west and the Strait of Salamis in the east) and elsewhere wider ones (the Gulf of Eleusis in the north). The eastern straits, opposite the homonymous ancient town, lies between the coastal area of Attica (modern Keratsini and Perama) and the island's coast, and terminates with the Cape of Kynosoura. The islet of Psyttaleia is found at the southern entrance of the passage, more or less in the center of the strait.

The protagonists' preparations and maneuvers prior to the battle

The Greeks' deliberations and decisions

The deployment of an enormous army of 350,000 men (many more than the standards of that time) and of a very powerful fleet of 700 ships (with estimated crews of over 140,000

The naval Battle of Salamis

AN AQUATIC SAKA EPIBATES (480 BC)
Regardless of the nationality of the epibatae *(marines) that served in every fleet squadron of the Persian Empire, every ship carried a unit of trusted Iranian warriors (Persians, Medes, or Sakas) that supervised the crew's behavior and morale. The marine illustrated here belongs to the Saka race and is a part of an elite unit, as denoted by the decorated* mesomphalion *(shield boss) of his Boetian style shield, whereas the linear patterns on his uniform denote his unit or clan. The Saka marines were recruited from riparian areas and were, therefore, among the few soldiers in the Persian imperial army that could swim, hence they were called the aquatic Sakas. (Uniform research and reconstruction - illustration by Christos Giannopoulos)*

An Assyrian-style copper Persian helmet, captured by the Greeks following the Battle of Marathon. (Archeological Museum of Olympia)

sailors) was not a simple course of operations for the Greek leaders. Many of them, taking into account the 3, 5, 10, or 20 ships under their command, looked awestruck at the astonishing squadrons of 100, 150, and 200 enemy ships. At Cape Artemisium, the weather had been particularly favorable to the Greeks, destroying ten times more ships than the Persians lost in the naval battle (600 Persian ships were lost through storms with just 60 to 70 losses in combat). Such a thing would be exceptionally unlikely, if not impossible, inside the relatively narrow Saronic Gulf. Moreover, the Greeks preferred to fight in an area of sea where their ground forces were close by onshore so they could offer mutual support. In the case of Salamis, however, the Greek fleet had to operate far from the army that was stationed on the Isthmus. Posted on the island were just a few units of Athenian soldiers (no more than 6,000 to 7,000 men) and a number of archers (at most 800). These had been brought from Crete by the Athenian leaders in time to be used on the ships. In contrast, the Persian army and fleet were in complete collaboration and accustomed to supporting and protecting each other.

Images of thousands of Athenian refugees carrying their meager belongings and, a while later, the smoke from the blazing city of Pallas Athena, had a tremendously adverse impact on the morale as well as the tactics of the Greek generals. Yet as is very often the case, and depending on a commander's personality and temperament, the same facts that may signify to one leader a threat to be avoided, can represent for another a challenge to be accepted. Most of the Greek governors, especially those from the Peloponnese, driven either by caution or defeatism, focused their thoughts mainly on the absence of the support by ground forces, something that would have been available if they had fallen back to the Isthmus of Corinth. There the entire army of the Greek allies (25,000 to 30,000 soldiers, most of them lightly armed) had been assembled under the leadership of the Spartan king Cleombrotus (brother of the hero of Thermopylae, Leonidas) and had hurriedly constructed a line of fortification. If the Greek fleet had arrayed in this area, it would cover the entire defensive line in case of any hostile landing on the indefensible eastern coast, shaping a solid front.

Themistocles, however, who dreamed of outdoing the Marathon victory scored by Miltiades (who had saved his home city and the whole of Greece - "Miltiades' trophy"), saw the perfect opportunity to crush the Asian intruders in the familiar area of Salamis. Fortunately, a few years earlier the democratic party had prepared the Athenian municipality for such a possibility and put into effect a grandiose naval program involving the construction of 200 triremes and the training of the Athenians in naval combat. There was no way Themistocles would allow this incredible opportunity to be lost due to the objections of certain narrow-minded Greeks.

Contrary to similar experiences in the past, the Greek states that now rallied against the common enemy had actually entrusted the management of the naval operations to a collective leadership. The Spartan general Eurybiades, son of Eurycleides, was the formal commander-in-chief. The role of this particular leader, who was only directly in command of the 16

The naval Battle of Salamis

A charging Athenian hoplite. A depiction on a stele at the Athenian Acropolis. (Museum of Acropolis)

Spartan ships, was rather strange, as he had other, more experienced generals with more powerful naval forces under his command. Themistocles led the 180 Athenian ships; Adeimantus commanded the 40 from Corinth, while another general led the 42 vessels from Aegina. Under these conditions, Eurybiades' true role was more political than purely military. His primary mission was to balance and co-ordinate the views and divergent parochial attitudes of the other military governors. Although such a role might appear remarkable by today's standards, it was however a reality. The Greek leaders, of whom there were at least 15 most important ones, each commanded squadrons of three or more ships and participated on equal terms on the council of the co-generals with one vote for each of them. Themistocles, who commanded 180 ships, had one vote, as did the governor of Eretria with seven vessels, the general from Leukas with three ships, and so on. It is unknown if those in command of just a single ship also participated. Given the Greek lust for power and egocentricity, one understands how difficult it must have been for Eurybiades to chair these councils. He was, nevertheless, more than capable of coping with this challenging role, as he managed to ensure that all the decisions were made on schedule, and saw to it that they were carried out by everyone.

Under the pressure, therefore, of the critical circumstances and the dramatic sight of the smoke still rising from the blazing temples on the Acropolis – and, indeed, after a long, heated discussion – the prevailing opinion of the leaders' council, convened by Eurybiades, was that the fleet should retreat to Corinthia where it could be near the army and that the naval battle with Persia would therefore be fought there. Themistocles, however, as a genuine democratic leader, visited his compatriot governors of the Athenian triremes and discussed the plan with them; they all agreed (Mnesiphilus' opinion is especially noted in the sources and it seems that the Athenian crews generally adopted it) that they should remain and fight where they were, while in sight of their burning houses and temples. In the event of the fleet sailing, they feared that there would be a serious possibility that the (up to that point) united Greek allied fleet could disband. With the support of his fellow-citizens (who constituted almost the half of the Greek force, approximately 36,000 soldiers out of a total of almost 75,000) and feeling that he expressed actual Greek national interests, Themistocles, now with steely determination, appeared before Eurybiades and requested that he reconvene the martial council. The latter, obviously appreciating not only the Athenian general's experience, but also his naval force of 180 ships, promptly called the council together for a second time. There, the animated Themistocles immediately began speaking, fervently setting out to the at least 14 attending generals the advantages of a naval engagement in the narrow passage of Salamis. This sudden, irregular initiative irritated a number of the generals and it seems that Adeimantus of Corinth (commander of 40 Corinthian ships) exchanged harsh words with Themistocles. The latter, however, having calmed down, as Herodotus relates, addressed Eurybiades, actually directing the following words to everyone at the meeting: "Today, it is in your hands to save Greece if you listen to me and remain here in order to fight a naval battle, and if you are not convinced by the words of those who want you to move the ships to Isthmus. Listen to the two plans and compare them. If you fight at Isthmus, you will fight in open sea, which is not in our best interests and you will lose Salamis, Megara, and Aegina, even if we have luck on our side. The barbarian army will follow the navy and, thus, you yourself will lead them to the Peloponnese and you will place entire Greece at risk. If, however, you do what I propose, you will have the following advantages: firstly, we will fight in a narrow place with our own few ships against many more, and if the result of this battle is the one that appears most likely, we will win a glorious victory. Because fighting in a narrow location is in our favor, while it will be in our opponents' favor if we fight in a wide location... And the greatest advantage is that you will fight in the same way for the Peloponnese if you remain here, as if you fought at Isthmus. If you think wisely, you will not bring the enemy to strike the Peloponnese..." (*History, Bk. viii*)

Themistocles had spoken correctly from a military viewpoint. Except for the obvious advantages that the smaller Greek forces would have fighting in a narrow location, from a strategic viewpoint it is always preferable to fight a battle away from your main territories rather than with your back against the wall, no matter how favorable that might appear from the standpoint of morale and the power of despair. In this particular case, leading their opponents to the area of Isthmus, where the Greeks would undeniably have an advantage as far as a ground battle was concerned, did not reverse the obvious disadvantage of a naval battle in the open seas of the Saronic Gulf. A

The naval Battle of Salamis

SICYONIAN EPIBATES (480 BC)
The typical Greek epibates (marine) of the 5th Century BC carried just elementary defensive armor (shield and helmet), so that he could safely swim in the event that the ship on which he served was sunk. His offensive weapon was a heavy one-edged cutting sword, a typical weapon during the Persian wars. (Uniform research and reconstruction - illustration by Christos Giannopoulos)

confrontation on the open sea would allow the larger fleet to outflank and encircle the smaller, with obvious adverse consequences for the latter.

The Peloponnesian generals, who wished to redeploy at Isthmus possessed very limited strategic horizons. They were imbued with the landsman's attitude and their thinking was defensive and leaning toward the pessimistic. It was characteristic that their counter-argument was that, in the event of defeat, the crews could be easily salvaged near Kenchreai (entry of Isthmus from the side of the Saronic Gulf), and could, therefore, take refuge on the neighboring land. The Athenian admiral, nevertheless, thought in terms of victory and not in terms of a possible rescue after an expected defeat.

Despite the Athenian admiral's logical and militarily correct arguments, some Peloponnesians still disagreed. The most powerful of all, Adeimantus, the commander of the Corinthian squadron (the second largest after that of Athens), dared to offend Themistocles by making a statement particularly designed to hurt him the most. He pointed out that the Athenian admiral was "homeless," as Athens had already been conquered and, as such, he should have no right to speak and his proposals should not be put to the vote. Themistocles, however, having been used to personal recriminations at the Athenian Municipal assembly, readily and cogently replied that the Athenians' new homeland was "their 200 ships" with which they could set sail to Sicily and establish another homeland. Moreover, this was precisely what they would do if the fleet did not fight in Salamis. The threat was serious. If the Athenians withdrew, the Greek fleet would remain with 202 ships and the Peloponnesian leaders would continue arguing. Realizing the awkward situation, the formal commander-in-chief Eurybiades sided with Themistocles and made clear to the other wayward generals that it was preferable to fight in the advanced position in which they had arrayed their 382-ship fleet rather than near their homelands with a fleet of 202 or even fewer, given that the leaders of Megara (20 ships), Aegina (30), Chalkis (20) and Eretria (7), whose homelands would remain completely defenseless, might follow the Athenians. Curiously, the final decision was unanimous. They would all fight, willingly or not, at Salamis. This, however, was not enough for Themistocles. In order to avoid any sudden reversal of the decision, he devised an ingenious and daring plan, worthy of a great, decisive yet unscrupulous leader (certainly where national interests were concerned). As the other generals wanted to fight with their backs against the wall, he would give them the chance. He fully briefed and sent Siccinus, his Asian slave and teacher of his children, who also knew Persian, to the court of the Persian king. Siccinus revealed to the Persian dignitaries (not to Xerxes himself) the "supposedly" favorable attitude of the Athenian leader and the Greek plans, and the fact that they had decided to retreat with low morale to the Peloponnese the following day. A way of action was not indicated in the message, this being left to the Persian leadership. It was not as strange as it might appear that the information from Themistocles was totally believable and that the Persian plans were changed so that they would keep up with the Greek fleet, cut off its retreat, and finally fight the battle at Salamis. As the Persians were already aware of the Greek political divisions

The naval Battle of Salamis

The route taken by the Persian expeditionary force in 480 BC.

and their lust for power, it was quite conceivable that certain Greek leaders would defect, as a hostile advance appeared inevitable. Had not the Macedonians, the Thessalians, the Phthiots, the Boeotians, etc., already done something similar?

It was this bold action, which of course involved a high degree of danger due to the smoldering suspicion and disputes among the Greek leaders, that made of Themistocles the first leader in world military history known to have successfully applied a strategy of indirect approach. Since then, Greek political and military leaders have often used such stratagems.

The Persians' deliberations and decisions

The Persian commanders, under the strict supervision of Xerxes, had thoroughly studied the location and realized the disadvantages of a potential confrontation with the Greeks in the narrow area from the moment they had reached and anchored in Phaleron Bay. Thus, they did not attempt to harass them for days but instead opted to observe them in an effort to understand their intentions. They had more ships that were taller and possessed higher speed; ships, in other words, eminently suitable for fighting in the open sea. These characteristics, however (numerical supremacy and speed), would be wasted or converted into a disadvantage (the tall construction) in the event that they fought in a narrow area like that at Salamis.

It appears that the initial decision of the Persian king was to reach Salamis overland. Once there, he would fill the narrow passage with soil from the current coast of Amphiali to the island that today is called Hagios Georgios. This plan, even if it was not technically impossible, was prevented because the Greeks patrolled with experienced archers on their ships and effectively harassed the work of the Persian engineers and workers.

Apollo's temple at Corinth. Representatives from the Greek cities that had decided to resist the Persian invader gathered on the outskirts of Corinth.

The naval Battle of Salamis

A PHOENICIAN MARINE (480 BC)
The Phoenicians were the largest and most reliable and experienced naval force in the service of the Achaemenians. According to Herodotus and depictions in Phoenician artworks, their marines wore Greek-style crested helmets, padded linen or leather breastplates, and carried round shields and javelins. Apart from that, the warrior illustrated here also carries one of the characteristic "naval" weapons of the eastern Mediterranean, the dorydrepanon *(spearshaft). To complete his array of arms he also carries a recurved sabre – the Asian equivalent of the Greek* machaera *or* kopis. *(Uniform research and reconstruction - illustration by Christos Giannopoulos)*

The ruins of the old amphitheater of Dionysus, at the base of the Acropolis, a little further down than the later Herodes' theater. According to ancient tradition, this theater was decorated with the two statues of Miltiades and Themistocles.

Xerxes' next idea was to divide his fleet into two great squadrons and leave one supervising the Greek naval force at Salamis while the other simultaneously sailed parallel to his ground forces against the Greek defensive line of Isthmus. Achaemenes, also a son of Darius and admiral of the Persian fleet, opposed this idea with the reasonable counter-argument that they would thus lose their numerical supremacy. With a total of almost 700 operational ships, the Persians were superior, an advantage they would lose if they separated their fleet into two equal squadrons of 350 ships each. If, on the other hand, they divided their fleet into two unequal parts, for example one with 200 ships with orders to head for the coasts of the Peloponnese while the other with 500 ships remained to keep an eye on the Greek fleet, they would be in constant danger of a surprise maneuver by the Greeks, hidden from their view by the island's mountains. The Greeks might, for example, spring out and crush the smaller Persian squadron and then return to their protected positions. Operations of this sort could whittle down the royal Persian force that, in any case, could not remain much longer in Attica now that winter was approaching.

Being in an awkward position, Xerxes and his admirals knew full well that in order to win the war they had to crush the powerful Greek fleet. But they dared not attempt such a venture inside the narrow passage where the opponent had the advantage. They had to force the Greeks to come out into the open sea and attack them there, though how they were to achieve this still remained a problem. The Persians were in a strategic dilemma and, being unable to make a decision, remained depressed and idle. Artemisia, Queen of Halicarnassus, stood out among the royal Persian military leaders, not only because she was a woman but also because she believed that they should let the Greek fleet disperse by itself, due to the supposed discord among the Greek leaders.

Siccinus found the Persian court in this deadlock and announced his secrets. Xerxes, who was desperately seeking a solution, seized the opportunity, as something similar had also happened at Thermopylae when Ephialtes had arrived with his information. Xerxes therefore ordered what he had not dared do for several days: the advance of his naval forces to Salamis, in order to compel the Greek fleet to do battle. Simultaneously, he ordered that the Egyptian squadron (100 to 150 ships at that time) be detached from his fleet and dispatched to cut off the western side of the island of Salamis – that is, the passage of Megara – so as to prevent the Greek naval forces from escaping. The other dignitaries seemed to concur, driven

The naval Battle of Salamis

either by voluntary agreement or servility. Once again, the only exception was Artemisia who boldly clung to her opinion. But the supreme master of the Asiatic forces had already made his decision and hurried to put it into effect.

The king's officers, encouraging their soldiers and sailors with decisive commands and continued optimism, boarded their ships and slowly set sail on a moonless night (27th to 28th or 28th to 29th of September), from Phaleron to the eastern entrance of the narrow area. There they arrayed their fleet on both sides of Psyttaleia Island and, following Xerxes' orders, disembarked 4,000 elite soldiers who set up camp on the shore. Their mission was to monitor the approaching clash, capture any enemies who managed to swim to that point as well as to rescue any Asians. Also putting the royal plan into effect, the Egyptian squadron of 100 to 150 ships sailed quickly to cut off the exit from the passage of Megara.

Following these moves, the Greeks found themselves surrounded in Salamis with no option but to stay and fight. By means of their successful night maneuver, the Persians had surrounded the Greeks, but the crews of their ships were forced to spend the night at their posts, in contrast to their enemies who had rested in their camp on the land, conserving their strength for the crucial battle on the following day. According to the ancient sources, the Greek generals were informed of the Persian encircling movement that had been carried out under the moonless night, while they remained in council. Themistocles' aristocratic Athenian rival Aristeides, the son of Lysimachus and an exile on Aegina, brought the news of the Persian move. He had spotted the Persians and hurried to inform the Greek camp and also to side with his country's leaders. This fact was also confirmed by the men on the trireme of Tenos (or, according to Plutarch, of Tenedos) under Panaitios. That evening they seized the opportunity to defect to their compatriots' side, with whom they lined up and fought the next day.

The great naval Battle (28th or 29th September 480 BC)

Early in the morning of the crucial day, the 550 to 600 ships of the royal Persian fleet, crowded next to each other and in position facing north, were able to see a number of the Greek ships drawn up on the sandy beaches of Salamis. Hindering each

A statue of a man carrying a calf, an Athenian's dedication to the goddess Athena. This statue, mutilated, as were all the others on the Acropolis, was discovered by the Athenians when they returned after the victory at Salamis. (Museum of Acropolis)

The trireme Olympias *under sail, thus allowing the rowers to rest.*

other because of their great numbers, the final Persian array deployed from east to west as follows:

The powerful Phoenician squadron (200 to 250 boats), under the command of Admiral Ariamenes, which was the most experienced and well versed in naval warfare, occupied the right flank. The barbarian squadrons of Caria (commanded by Histaios and Pigres), of Cilicia (commanded by Syennesis), of Lycia (commanded by Cyberniscus and Tharybe), of Pamphylia, and of the Cyprus Greeks (in total almost 200 ships) were positioned in the center of the Persian formation. On the left were the Greeks of Ionia (commanded by Theomestor, son of Androdamas), of Thrace, and of Pontus (150 to 200 ships). They were also under the command of admiral Ariabignes, son of Darius.

As soon as the sun rose, everyone could clearly see the Persian naval force at the entrance to the narrow channel. This alarmed the Greek fleet and the seamen, after having breakfast, assembled according to their cities and received orders from their military commanders. The generals made patriotic speeches stressing the importance of the oncoming conflict to their soldiers. Themistocles addressed the Athenian squadron, which was the largest (at least 36,000 men), delivering a speech that his contemporaries considered to be the most passionate and crucial, even though historians did not save it.

The penteconter, a warship with 50 oars (sweeps) in total (25 on each side). It carries an embolon, *which was actually the ending to the bow and, therefore, it was a wooden addition, not copper, like those on the triremes. The Greeks used 14 of these ships at Salamis. (Maritime Museum of Piraeus)*

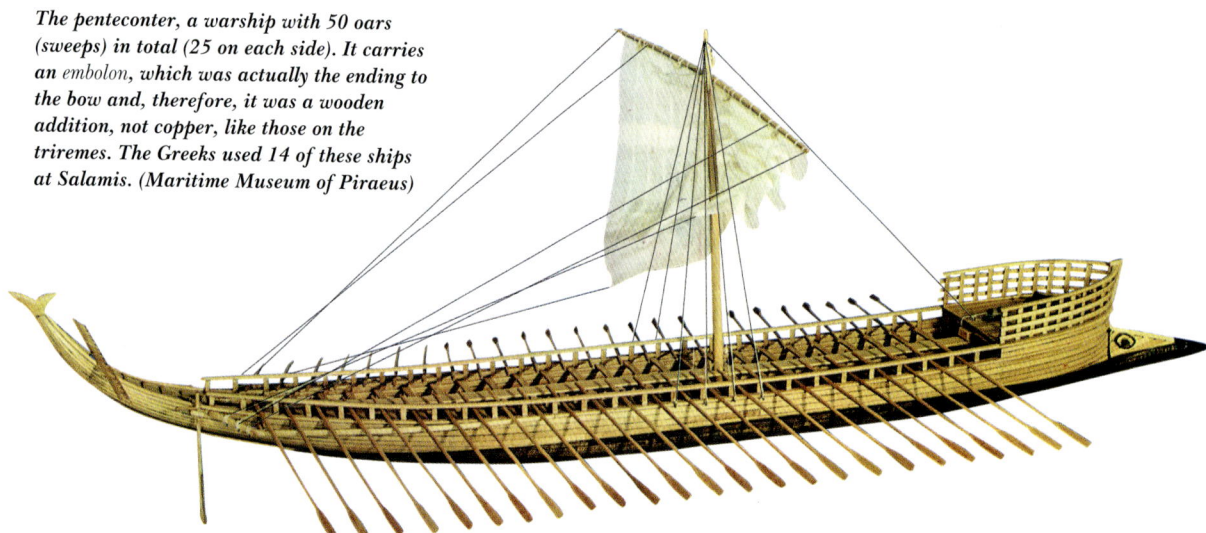

The naval Battle of Salamis

GREEK EPIBATAE AT THE NAVAL BATTLE OF SALAMIS (480 BC)
In the illustration are depicted i) a Corinthian epibates *(marine) wearing a patterned helmet and carrying a hoplite shield with Pegasus on a red background as an emblem (Pegasus was the horse of the Corinthian hero Bellerophon, who slaughtered the Asian demon of death, Chimaera, a symbolism directly relevant to the historical period of the great battle) and ii) an Aeginian* epibates *wearing a white tunic with a leather* spolas *(robe) over his breastplate and carrying a hoplite sword, a Corinthian helmet and a hoplite shield decorated with a sea turtle on a white background. The Aeginians constituted a considerable force in the Mediterranean; their merchant ships sailed to all eastern harbors, their currency had great market value and their battle-trained navy, according to Herodotus, played a highly significant role during the Battle of Salamis. The sea turtle, used as an emblem on Aeginian coins, demonstrates the island's supremacy both on land and at sea. (Uniform research and reconstruction - illustration by Christos Giannopoulos)*

Herodotus only remarked, "the entire speech was a comparison between the best and the worst and talked about what is related with a man's innate capacities and the situations that he confronts in his life. He thus urged the warriors to prefer the best of the above..." The fact that Themistocles' speech was not recorded made its later mythical embellishment easy, after, of course, the favorable outcome of the battle.

It is not recorded in any existing source, but there is no doubt that the reference to Leonidas' heroic sacrifice and to the Pan-Hellenic character of the battle that he and his soldiers fought at Thermopylae, contributed the most to raising the morale of the allied Greek forces.

The exhortative orations over, the Greek crews (almost 75,000 men) took up their positions in a climate of patriotic exaltation and widespread enthusiasm. Obviously, the presence of crowds of civilians next to the anchored warships also contributed greatly to the prevailing atmosphere, reminding the warriors of their duty either explicitly with words or implicitly just by their silent presence, as refugees on the coast, the distress showing on the faces of the old men, women, and children). Particularly for the Athenians, who knew that most of the civilians were refugees from Attica, as a modern writer, G. Psaroulaki, has cogently remarked: "it was indeed a critical battle, a struggle for freedom and survival according to them: if they were defeated, they would no longer have a homeland. They could not rely on Xerxes' compassion and they knew that defeat meant the annihilation of Athens as an independent city and most probably of themselves. The flames of the burning city of Pallas were nothing compared to those that burned in the hearts of the Athenian fighters." Those pent-up emotions, the sense of patriotic duty, the awareness of the historical responsibility that burdened the shoulders of those people, the working people of the cities and the countryside, the craftsmen and retailers, who literally held the fate of their cities in their hands for the first time, was recorded most successfully in the paean that Aeschylus put in the Greek seamen's mouths:

"Advance, ye sons of Greece, from thralldom save your country, save your wives, your children save, the temples of your gods, the sacred tomb where rest your honour'd ancestors; this day the common cause of all demands your valor."

The Greek battle array, with the ships being deployed in the sea from north to south, was as follows: the

Bronze statuette of a Greek hoplite. His posture implies that he might possibly be either in the phalanx or on the deck of a trireme.

The naval Battle of Salamis

A current view of the Salamis strait. (Photo by E. Tsakirakis)

powerful Athenian squadron (180 ships), under the command of Themistocles, was on the left. In the center were the triremes of all the small states (Chalcis, Eretria, Sicyon, and others). In the place of honor, on the right of the array, the Spartan squadron under the command of Eurybiades (who was nominally the commander-in-chief of the Greek fleet) sided with that of Megara (20 ships) and of Aegina (30 ships), and maybe with other smaller units. The precise array of the Greek naval force is not totally clear, however, and the position of some of the contingents remains obscure. In particular, the location of the Corinthian squadron (the second greatest in the Greek force with 40 ships), is uncertain. Nevertheless, there is no doubt that the most powerful wing in the Greek battle array was on the left (the Athenian squadron) and, apparently, this one would bear most of the weight of the battle.

The warships of both arrays were of the same type, almost all of them being triremes. There were, however, a number of fundamental differences. All the ships of the Persian array, whether barbarian or Greek, had a full deck, covering the entire length and width of the ship, with raised prows and sterns, in contrast to the Greek vessels that did not have full decks and were, in consequence, lower. The Persian fleet's ships, with their through decks and tall prows and sterns, sailed better in the open seas, and were faster. (According to Konstantinos Rados, this advantage was due to the timber and the Asiatic shipyards' construction techniques). At the same time though, the Persian fleet's warships were more vulnerable to lateral winds, their greater height and weight leaving them more exposed. The Greek ships appeared simpler and more primitive, with fewer comforts. They were slower but they were not so vulnerable to lateral winds coming from gulfs and bays, as they were lower in the water and, consequently, less exposed. The Persian ships were also much more spacious: they could easily embark 30 or even 40 soldiers, who took up their positions on the deck. In contrast, the Greeks usually had just 10 soldiers aboard most states' triremes, although the Athenian ships could carry more

A municipality of Ampelakia poster, printed on the occasion of the celebration of the anniversary of the Battle of Salamis. (Photo by E. Tsakirakis)

(a total of 18: 14 soldiers and 4 archers). Nevertheless, the increased manpower of the Persian ships did not give the positive result expected by the Persian leaders (this being increased firepower during ship-to-ship engagements), since the additional weight made the ships harder to control and less maneuverable. This disadvantage was increased by the unexpected sea swell, a local phenomenon of which the Persians were unaware.

When the squadron leaders gave the signal, the whole Greek fleet headed for the enemy. In the beginning, the rowing was not energetic as the Greeks tried to save their strength before engaging the foe. Immediately afterwards they began to give way, although still facing forward. That is, they sailed backwards, rowing in the opposite direction. This maneuver, which was quite difficult for crews that were not perfectly trained, was put into effect in an obviously dissimilar way. This was inevitable as the crews from the Greek cities had different levels of training. Moreover, when this movement was performed, it appears that the powerful Corinthian squadron (40 triremes under Adeimantus' command) played a special role, although what it was is unknown. Most probably, they sailed north and, from an initial right flank location, they finally took up positions in the center of the Greek battle array. Whatever the case, the conscious dissimilarity in the performance of the maneuver as well as the maneuver itself, was undertaken by the Greek admirals in order to gain time and to draw the Persians into the narrow part of the channel (between the island of Hagios Georgios and Cape Kynosoura). Meanwhile, Xerxes and his advisers, watching from a panoramic position on Mount Aegaleo, had the impression that the Greeks' morale was low and, consequently, they were an easy prey for the overconfident royal Persian fleet. The direct result of this was that the whole of the royal entourage was filled with optimism; so much so that Xerxes commanded his fleet to enter the narrow area and attack the Greek ships fiercely. When the command arrived (by messengers on ships that had been specially detached for this purpose), the whole of the royal fleet of 550 to 600 ships quickly sailed to the north and deployed along the coastline (within the narrow passage) across a front of almost three kilometers, from Perama (where the leading Phoenician ships had arrayed) up to Cape Kynosoura. So it was that Themistocles' plan was beginning to take shape: the Persians were now inside the narrow passage and facing west ready for the engagement. The epic battle had finally begun.

The Battle

Upon seeing that their opponents were in the narrow passage and moving aggressively against them, all the Greek commanders, who were still standing by and had covered almost

The naval Battle of Salamis

half of the distance, ordered their crews to advance and attack "at full speed." According to tradition, the signal for the attack was the cry "Madmen, how far will ye yet back your ships?" which spread along the entire battle line. Even if that cry does not appear very practical when compared to a typical trumpet call, it nevertheless impelled the Greek crews to row hard and propel their ships aggressively against the enemy line, clearly demonstrating that the Persians' impression concerning the Greeks' low morale was without foundation.

The Athenians' 180 triremes on the left, keeping close to the islet of Hagios Georgios to prevent any chance of being outflanked, moved rapidly and first attacked the 200 to 250 triremes of the Phoenicians, who were arrayed on the right flank of the Persian battle line. The impact between these two forces was the one that decided the outcome of the naval battle. According to Diodorus Siculus, Ameinias' ship from Dekeleia (near Athens) first rammed the leading Phoenician ship and destroyed it and, because the Athenian trireme's ram stuck in the enemy ship, the Greek *epibatae* (marines) were able to attack and wipe out the Persians on the stricken vessel. With this single action, the Phoenicians ran out of luck, because right at the outset of the battle, they had already lost both their flagship and their leader, Admiral Ariamenes, who was killed after fighting heroically while taking part in the assault on the Greek ship. Following this, and with the help of other Athenian ships that, in the meantime, had caught up, Ameinias' trireme broke free from the stricken enemy vessel and vigorously set about attacking other ships. At the same time, other Athenian vessels successfully attacked the Phoenician ships that had advanced ahead of the rest. In another instance, the trireme of the Athenian Lycomedes, showing exceptional seamanship, sliced off the sumptuous prow decoration of a hostile ship and captured it. At this juncture of the battle, the Greek ships applied the tactics of *diekplous* (breakthrough and ram), which the Phoenicians found very difficult to combat successfully, as their crowded, overloaded ships could not be stabilized in the narrow passage and thus form a compact front or maneuver to avoid the skillful Athenian commanders' attacks. Their situation was made even worse by the apparent inability to name a replacement for the dead commander Ariamenes, a fact that clearly reveals the problem of the Persian high command. No other capable tactician immediately took charge, creating a situation that Diodorus succinctly described: "The barbarian navy was confused, because those giving orders were too many and none of them gave the same orders." The Phoenicians, however, were unfazed even if the beginning of the battle had not gone their way. They were experienced, capable seamen and they were aware that Xerxes was watching from his throne on the slopes of Mount Aegaleo; they also knew that he

A bronze shield (probably used for ceremonial purposes and not for battle) along with a bronze bell-shaped breastplate. (Olympia Museum)

primarily relied upon them and for that reason they strenuously attempted to turn the tide of the battle in their favor. Time, however, was passing and, at around 9:00 a.m., the southern wind that was very well known to the Greeks of that region, started to blow and raise waves to a swell. The Persian commanders, who were unaware of this phenomenon, were all caught off guard and soon began to sheer away, losing their forward course and exposing their vulnerable sides to the attackers, who did not miss the opportunity to ram them. The ferocious naval battle now covered most of the narrow sea passage. Wishing to stress the paramount importance of the wind, Diodorus remarks, "As the rowers could not do their job, many of the Persian triremes turned sideways and were rammed again and again." At this stage of the battle, the Greeks had gained an important operational advantage. Their lower ships, being influenced less by the lateral wind, proved more effective than those of the Persians; as a result, their captains could direct them wherever they wished (either straight at an enemy vessel or plowing alongside through its oars, immobilizing it). In contrast, the Persian warships were now in an awkward position as, being higher in the water, they were more buffeted by the force of the wind, causing them to become unstable and hard to steer. The Persian ships' instability was only aggravated by the weight of the large number of men (30 to 40 soldiers) aboard. In these conditions, the Greeks were able to gain the upper hand and, as time passed, they became even more aggressive, striking the enemy with increasing ferocity. The Persians were in such a state of confusion that several ships collided with each other in their struggle to maneuver.

Eventually, the Phoenicians, who were now under immense pressure, either by command – or, more likely, the lack of it – turned about and began to head south in an attempt to escape the stranglehold imposed by the Athenian ships. But because of the confined space and the intense pressure combined, probably, with fear, what began as a tactical redeployment created confusion among the squadrons of the disparate fleet and quickly led to a generalized rout.

Beset with these problems, the

Model of an Athenian trireme of the 5th century BC. It was constructed on behalf of the Maritime Museum of the Aegean by C. Simonides, and based on plans of J. Coates. The Olympias trireme reconstruction was also based on these plans.

The naval Battle of Salamis

The area where it is believed that the monument commemorating the Salamis warriors once stood. (Photo by E. Tsakirakis)

Phoenician ships moved in an uncoordinated way with the inevitable result that some of them careered into each other (which left them, of course, at the mercy of the attackers), and forced the following ships no other option but to try to maneuver out of their way. The result of all these disorganized efforts was the breakup of the battle line, allowing the massed entry of the Athenian ships into the Phoenician array. The latter resisted as long as they were able but it soon became apparent that any individual effort was insufficient compared to the determination and fighting spirit of the Athenians, who continued to engage the enemy with order and cohesion. At the same time, those ships that tried to slip away had difficulty moving, due to the great rush, even though they could in general out sail their pursuers. Other ships of the royal Persian force still moving westward became entangled with the Phoenician vessels that were heading south. Moreover, the confusion caused by vessels intent on escape and the sight of the powerful, but now dispirited, Phoenicians retreating shocked the royal fleet's entire battle array. Many Persians were filled with terror when they realized that their battle line's entire right flank, commanded by their most powerful contingent, had collapsed.

At the same time, the victorious Athenians, having pursued the Phoenicians, now turned to starboard in order to outflank the triremes in the Persian center and attack them from the rear. The Persian vessels came under terrible pressure and crews' morale plummeted as they faced enemies on all sides: the ships of the Greek center to the west, and the Athenians' warships to the north and east. Under these conditions, their battle line totally collapsed and from that point each ship attempted only to defend itself. The Greek triremes were easily able to pick their targets and struck decisively with their rams, crushing bulwarks, decks, timber, oars, and human bodies. The soldiers fought their own hard battle on the ships, throwing javelins and spears and shooting arrows. But when the ram of a hostile ship struck, very little could be done, as panic spread aboard the stricken vessel, flooding with sea water. Only well-trained crews could remain composed and manage to cope in such a difficult situation. But, within

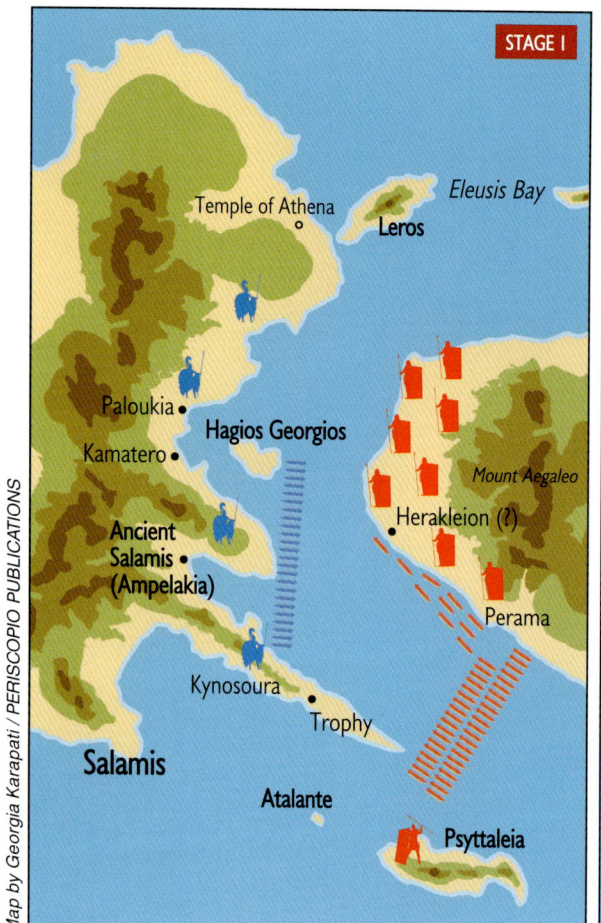

a multinational fleet with disparate squadrons – as the Persian fleet was – few such crews existed. Sometimes the stricken ships completely capsized and the men found themselves floundering in the sea. According to primary sources, during these dramatic moments, the citizens of Aegina proved to be unrivalled in inflicting enormous losses on their enemies. In fact, Polycritus of Aegina, in addition to Ameinias of Athens, were the foremost commanders during the battle.

That said, not all those who distinguished themselves during the battle were Greek. According to primary sources, some of the crews of the Persian ships demonstrated extraordinary bravery and fought hard despite the unforeseen course of the battle. The death of many leaders on the Persian side, including Ariamenes, Ariabignes, and Syennesis, while commanding their ships proves both their capability and their undeniable bravery. Among those who, in fact, fought with distinction, albeit unjustified, were the Ionians, who had sided with Xerxes against their compatriots. In mitigation, they explained that they wanted to avoid being accused of cooperating with their compatriots and, in consequence, betraying their tyrant-king. Moreover, they were afraid of possible retaliation against their families in Ionia if they did not demonstrate their loyalty. Xerxes himself took note of and applauded this "flawless" performance by the Ionian seamen in the narrow Strait of Salamis against their

The naval Battle of Salamis

THE BATTLE OF SALAMIS, 480 BC

- Greek fleet
- Persian fleet
- Greek forces
- Persian forces
- Immortals' squad

Stage I: the Persian fleet entered the Salamis strait during the night. The Greek fleet was arrayed for the battle occupying the area from the coast of Kynosoura up to Hagios Georgios islet.

Stage II: the Persian fleet was arrayed with the coast of Perama at its back. The Greeks attacked their opponents.

Stage III: the left wing of the Greek fleet, in which the Athenian squadron was arrayed, managed to outflank the Persian fleet and beat off the Phoenician ships that were directly opposite them.

Stage IV: many Persian ships abandoned the battle and, being pursued by the Greeks, found themselves trapped between Kynosoura and Psyttaleia and suffered severe losses.

compatriots. It is within character that, at some point, Phoenician seamen landed on the beach in front of Mount Aegaleo and approached the king's court to accuse the Ionians of supposed betrayal. Xerxes, however, who had seen everything, not only spurned these unfair accusations but punished the slanderers with death.

Despite the bravery demonstrated by the majority of Persian crews, the Greeks proved totally formidable, since their own motives were much more fundamental. Above all, the Athenians, as well as those from Aegina and Megara, surpassed themselves in skill and determination. They knew that defeat was not an option and fought – especially the Athenians – under the eyes of their families and friends who were on Salamis and anxiously watching the course of the battle. The fact that the Greeks were not tired, while the Persian crews had spent the previous night rowing, obviously played an important role as well.

Under these conditions, as time passed, more and more Persian ships retreated and attempted to flee the deadly embrace of the Greek triremes. At some point, either following orders or acting on their own initiative, all the Persian ships abandoned the conflict and hurried towards the southeastern exit of the strait in order to escape. A great number of ships managed to reach Phaleron Bay, where they redeployed. The vessels of the Egyptian squadron, which had not taken part in the battle, also sailed there later. The Greek crews, already victorious, intensified their efforts to limit the enemies' possibilities of escaping. Quite a few triremes and their captains distinguished themselves in this new role of the hunter, with Ameinias and Polycritus, once again, being among the most capable.

At sunset, with the sky taking the exquisite violet color of the Attic autumn, the last Persian escapees made for Phaleron, leaving the Greek ships in control of the naval battlefield, signifying the end of the momentous engagement. The Greek seamen, drunk with success, rescued as many castaways as they could and, obviously, finished off all the hostile ships that still remained afloat. At some point, probably during the afternoon, the Greek triremes rounded the islet of Psyttaleia, where they landed a party of soldiers and archers under the command of Aristeides of Athens. The Greeks attacked the Persian guard of 4,000 men that had been posted there before the battle and eliminated them after a short engagement. The Persian soldiers, who had themselves seen the result of the battle, were apparently not very optimistic as far as their future was concerned.

Themistocles' plan had succeeded beyond anyone's dreams. The high-spirited Greeks celebrated their victory both aboard their ships and on land and congratulated each other on their salvation. All of them fought to their utmost, but it was the Athenians, the first to come into contact with the formidable Phoenicians, who definitely deserved the greatest praise. Also, the Aeginians should be singled out for praise for the skill they exhibited throughout the conflict. The Corinthians' contribution to the battle as well as their exact location in the Greek battle array still remains an unanswered question, however. According to some, they had assumed the protection of the northern passages towards the Gulf of Eleusis to prevent the Egyptian ships from entering the battlefield and participating in the battle. But it seems unlikely that such a secondary role would be assigned to the second most powerful squadron of the Greek fleet, one that, furthermore, was particularly experienced as well as highly trained. Such a role could easily have been given to the 16 Spartan triremes or

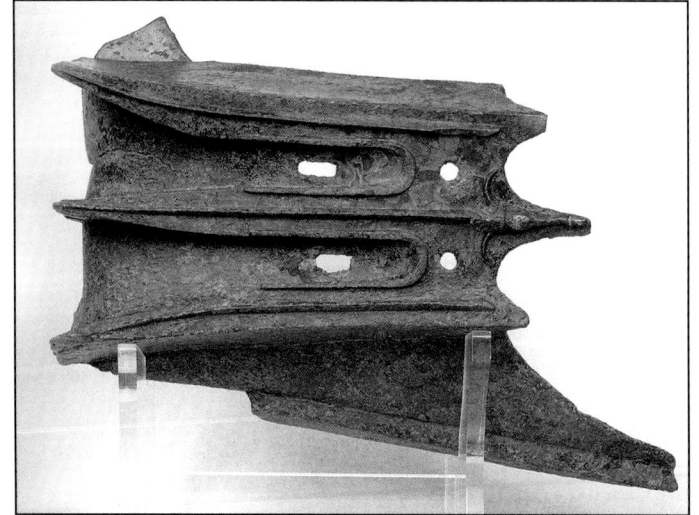

Bronze trireme embolon (ram). (Maritime Museum of Piraeus)

The naval Battle of Salamis

A marble plaque commemorating the bravery of the Corinthians who died during the Battle of Salamis. (Epigraphic Museum of Athens)

even to another squadron possessing even fewer ships. Besides, the Greeks could not have been caught off-guard by the Egyptian squadron, as they were in possession of all the island's coasts and were able to observe the enemies' actions and moves and could, accordingly, inform the Greek triremes in plenty of time. The distance between the passage of Megara, where the Egyptian squadron was posted, and the northern entry to the Salamis Strait, where the naval battle took place, is quite long, thus allowing a timely Greek deployment after receiving the appropriate signal. It was this favorable configuration of the battlefield that afforded the Greeks the opportunity of not detaching a large section of the fleet to guard against any potential threat by the Egyptians (thus maintaining the principle of saving energy), except, perhaps, for a few (possibly the Corinthian ones, but almost certainly, not all of them). Since neither the ancient references nor the various related sources mention the Egyptian ships, while in contrast, the bravery of the Corinthians is extensively cited, it can be concluded that the Egyptians demonstrated timidity and did not advance beyond the Passage of Megara, while the Corinthians took an active and determined part in the main battle. It may therefore be deduced that they were positioned in the center of the Greek battle array, close to the other Peloponnesians who were located on the right flank. The opposite premise would lead to the somewhat strange assumption that the Greek array had the characteristics of an unbalanced phalanx, with the 180 Athenian triremes on the left, which first attacked and defeated the opposing Phoenician force, while the center and right flanks followed with only a total of 148 triremes.

The losses of the naval Battle

Neither Herodotus nor Aeschylus mentioned the battle's losses; they both preferred to be vague about them, leaving the field open to all manner of exaggeration (such as claims of 500 Persian ships sunk). Ephorus, however, offers some figures that are accepted by modern historians. According to him, the defeated Persians lost at least 200 ships, either sunk or destroyed, while the victor's losses were just 40. A number of authors suspect that an unknown number of Persian ships may also have been captured, but this cannot be confirmed. Even if there were captures, they must have been too few for subsequent historians or the epic poets to mention them. These numbers, i.e., 200 Persian and 40 Greek vessels lost, appear reasonable and conform to the general course of the battle.

The Greek side, however, held another, very important advantage. Almost all Greek seamen knew how to swim and could reach friendly territory or survive until allied Greek triremes could rescue them. Consequently, of the 8,000 men who had the misfortune of falling into the Saronic Gulf (200 individuals on each of the 40 ships), fewer than half perished (1,000 to 2,000 men). On the other hand we should also take into account the unknown number of losses of those who were wounded on the ships that were not sunk. In contrast, according to ancient sources, the Persian fleet, the crews of which were unable to swim, mourned an enormous number of fighters who perished through drowning – the majority, in fact, of the 44,000 unfortunates who fell into the sea (an average of 220 individuals on each of the 200 ships). This is possibly an overestimation, especially as far as the sailors were concerned, particularly the Phoenicians and Ionians, but obviously true for those posted aboard ships as raiding forces, that is, the foot soldiers from the Iranian plateau. Of course, those Persians who managed to swim towards the coast of Salamis found Athenian soldiers waiting to kill them on the spot or, if fortunate, to capture them. In addition, the entire guard of 4,000 men posted on Psyttaleia were either killed or taken prisoner.

The final report reveals that the Persian forces suffered an overwhelming defeat. They lost one-third of their ships (at least 200 vessels) and a quarter of their crews (around 30,000 to 35,000 men), while the morale of the rest, including that of their leaders, collapsed.

A model of an advanced type of Greek trireme. The Ionians, who had sided with the Persians, probably had similar ones. (Maritime Museum of Piraeus)

The naval Battle of Salamis

ATHENIAN ARMORED HOPLITE (489 – 479 BC)
*According to Herodotus, the Athenian politician Aristeides commanded the Athenian hoplites that guarded the coasts of Salamis. Immediately after the end of the naval battle, he landed them on Psyttaleia Island where they eliminated the Persian squad that lay waiting to ambush any Greek castaways. In contrast to the usually unarmored epibatae on the trireme, the hoplites of the coastal guards were fully armored: they carried an Attic crested helmet, a composite breastplate made of furbished linen, leather and metal plates, bronze greaves, a hoplite shield, a thrusting spear and a double-edged sword. The emblem on his shield is the famous gorgoneion (Gorgon's head) painted here in the syle of the Attic workshops.
(Uniform research and reconstruction - illustration by Christos Giannopoulos)*

The consequences of the naval Battle

The Persian fleet's overwhelming defeat before the eyes of its supreme ruler, affected both the prestige and, above all, the morale of the Asiatic troops. In fact, it affected not only the morale of the lowly soldiers who suffered (as usual) all the unfavorable consequences of the battle (wounds, loss of close friends and colleagues, destruction of useful materials, etc.), but also the morale of their leaders. Xerxes himself was profoundly troubled about what he should do next, as he was in an awkward position due to the defeat and the imminent winter. His final decision, no doubt influenced by the precarious position in which he found himself, was to retire and let Mardonius resume hostilities the following year. It is more than probable that Siccinus played a very important role in this decision, taking into account Themistocles' indirect threats. In addition, it is certain that with his naval lines of communication and replenishment being cut off by the Greek fleet, the position of his army inside hostile territory with few resources looked particularly precarious.

By general consensus, in the event of a Persian victory at sea, the Greek world would have been in a desperate position. Considering the military and political information of the time, the attack on the Peloponnese would have been an easy affair, not, of course, from the protected Isthmus, but from an eastern beach that could easily have been approached by the Persians, who would have possessed naval supremacy from that point forward. General collapse would then have been only a matter of time. If this happened, with Greece becoming a subjugated country, as had happened with Ionia a few years earlier, all cultural creation would have stopped. Given, of course, our knowledge of Greek cultural achievements during the following centuries, one can only imagine the cataclysmic consequences for the entire world if that had occurred.

To the Greek people's great relief, a few days after the naval battle (that is, at the beginning of October 480 BC), the Persian army and fleet withdrew from Attica, whose residents returned to their homeland. Now, however, they were no longer the same people, the intimidated, grieving, gloomy refugees that had left with few belongings some weeks earlier, pinning all their hopes on the beliefs of a general. Instead, they were the proud, contented veterans of the Battle of Salamis. They were the ones who were present at a pivotal historic moment and who themselves wrote the history of their country's salvation both by their decisions and the hands that pulled with such determination on the long sweeps propelling their ships across the waves to that decisive victory.

The political importance of the naval Battle

Apart from the military consequences, the epic battle between the two naval forces in the sea off Salamis also had a great importance in other areas. In contrast to what was usual up to that time, fewer than 5,000 soldiers consisting of the relatively prosperous bourgeois and aristocrats, but more than 70,000 sailor/oarsmen *eretae*, belonging to economically and socially lower classes, inferior in prestige even to the thetae (wage earners and laborers) of the cities, took part in, and contributed to the Greek victory. This situation, which was understood by the contemporary citizens, lent (as it still does) a special political importance to the triumph. It was not just a victory of the Greeks over the Asian "barbarians"; it was also the victory of the simple, poor, free people over the servant/slaves of a monarch. It was the victory of democracy over despotism.

For the first time in history, the anonymous masses that constituted the disreputable *hoi polloi* (the "crowd"), squeezed in the narrow benches of the triremes and using their muscular strength and their morale as free men as weapons, actively participated to their utmost in this most decisive battle. The Greek maneuvers before and during the battle were successful, a fact that underlines the absolutely strict sailing discipline and the effective training that had preceded it. The Greek triremes were totally effective against the hostile fleet due to their skill and speed of maneuver. This combat efficiency showed that, on one hand, the ships' captains were fully in command and, on the other, that the oarsmen powering the ships were trying their utmost to achieve the necessary rhythm. The simple people handling the massive sweeps, sweating, next to, or on top of each other in somewhat unprotected positions, fought resolutely with indomitable courage and pride. Their role in achieving the great victory was decisive. And it was this knowledge of their contribution that raised the collective morale of the lower classes. Prior to the naval battle, they were the "crowd," the *hoi polloi*, usually without land or rights, to whom the landowning military men did not even entrust the defense of their homeland against cunning enemies. In the previous principal confrontation on the Plain of Marathon in 490 BC, it had been only the landowners who had formed the hoplites' phalanx. Then it was they who had won eternal glory. After the Battle of Salamis, this perception changed. From then on, it was the *hoi polloi* who had taken matters into their own hands with patience, tenacity, and discipline as their virtues, and under the skillful guidance of capable leaders (the most important of them having been elected), had triumphed over the "barbarians." The latter, no matter how bravely they fought at Salamis (and every source underlines this), and no matter how much they had been pressured by their despotic king, were defeated because they did not share the noble motives that mobilized the Greeks (defense of their freedom, homeland, family, way of life, and dignity).

The modern historian Alexandros Despotopoulos sums up in a few forceful words the values and ideals of the victors of Salamis: "The free citizens of the Greek cities, in which freedom along with courage were the supreme values, fought for their gods' altars and their homes with bravery and self-denial."

This modern monument in honor of the warriors of Salamis commemorates the marines, not the oarsmen, who were the actual heroes of the battle. (Photo by E. Tsakirakis)

44 *Salamis*

EGYPTIAN EPIBATES (MARINE) IN PERSIAN SERVICE (480 BC)

According to Herodotus, "...the Egyptians wore plated helmets and were armed with wide, hollow shields with broad rims and spears suitable for a naval battle...they wore breastplates and had long swords." The plated helmets and breastplates reported by the "father of history" were made from square pieces of linen or leather sewn together giving the impression of a relief surface. The cuirass depicted here is not the common linen one worn in the Achaemenian navy, but rather an Egyptian invention made of durable crocodile skin. The "long sword" reported by Herodotus, is probably the long double-edged sword with the Scythian-Persian cornuted handle depicted in the Persepolis Palace that was carried by the Great King's Egyptian or Indian subjects. Herodotus calls the long linen robe with the red fringes kalasiris *and the companies of Egyptian or Ethiopian marines* kalasirians. *(Uniform research and reconstruction - illustration by Christos Giannopoulos)*

The naval Battle of Salamis 45

CYPRIOT OR ASIAN DORIAN IN PERSIAN SERVICE (480 BC)
Herodotus gives an ambiguous description of the Cypriot *epibatae* (marines), whereas, as far as the Asian Dorians are concerned, he just reports that they used Greek weapons. Consequently, the unusual military attire shown here is from a Phoenician jewel made in Sardinia in 480 BC, explicitly depicting a Greek hoplite wearing a Corinthian helmet, composite Greek-Cypriot-style breastplate, greaves and an extraordinary human face shaped shield, probably portraying a satyr or even Pan. The trapezoid shape of the shield, which followed the anatomy of the human face, made it ideal for throwing a javelin. His offensive weapons were the *ancient Greek scimitar*, as English speaking archeologists named it, which was often used on continental Greece as a substitute for the *recurved sword* or the *kopis*. It is widely believed that both of them, however, along with the composite linen breastplates, are elements of Asian origin, which were copied from the Greeks during the late 6th Century BC.
(Uniform research and reconstruction - illustration by Christos Giannopoulos)

The "Wooden Walls"
Themistocles' stratagem

"He, therefore, consulted them to be prepared for a naval battle, this would be the wooden walls. This was the interpretation given by Themistocles and the Athenians considered that it was more correct than the interpretation of the soothsayers, who did not want to let them give a naval battle..."

Herodotus mentions the prophecies that the Athenians requested and received from the Oracle of Delphi, concerning the confrontation with the impending Persian danger, in the seventh book, entitled *Polhymnia*, of his monumental *Histories*.

The initial prophecy given by the Delphic Oracle's presiding priestess, known as the Pythia, disappointed the Athenian delegation. The Pythia, whose name is given as Aristonike, urged the Athenians to abandon their city, because she had foreseen its destruction: "Wretched ones, why sit you here? Flee and begone to remotest ends of earth, leaving your homes, high places in circular city; For neither the head abides sound, nor the body; Nor at bottom do the feet stay firm, nor the hands, Nor does the middle remain uninjured. All is lost. Fire pulls all down, and sharp Ares, driving his Syrian-bred horses. Many a fortress besides, and not yours alone shall he ruin. Many the temples of god to devouring flames he shall consign. There they stand now, the sweat of terror streaming down them. They quake with fear; from the rooftops black blood pours in deluging torrents. They have seen the coming destruction, and evil sheerly constraining. Get you gone out of the adyton! Blanket your soul with your sorrows." Then Timon, son of Androboulos, whom Herodotus describes as an important citizen of Delphi, advised the Athenians to request a second oracle, but this time as pleaders. The Athenians obeyed, and the Pythia gave them a more hopeful oracle: "Zeus of Olympus cannot be bent by Athena, even though she begs him with many words full of wisdom; but still I will tell you these words, solid as a diamond. When those that Cecrops names will be conquered and as many deep caves Kithairon has, then all-seeing Zeus will give the Third born of the Gods (goddess Athena) a wooden wall, the only unassailable one, in order to save you and your children. Do not wait tranquil for the cavalry and the large army coming from the land, but retreat, turning your back and the time to fight will come. Divine Salamis, you will be responsible for the loss of children, when Demeter's fruits will be seeded or reaped."

The second oracle eased somewhat the worries of the Athenian emissaries, who recorded it and returned to their city to announce it. The announcement of the oracle provoked different interpretations, however. What puzzled the Athenians in particular was the expression "wooden walls." Two interpretations prevailed. On one hand, the oldest citizens interpreted the "wooden walls" phrase as meaning fortifications. Indeed, a wooden wall had protected the Acropolis of Athens in the past, so they felt that the oracle was telling them to take cover behind it and resist from there.

The opposing view was that the "wooden walls" signified ships.

According to this interpretation, the Athenians had to ignore any other form of resistance on land and resort to the sea supported by their fleet. Those advocating resistance on the Acropolis disagreed, however, and warned the others that if the Athenians relied solely on their fleet, they would be destroyed, for the oracle had said: "Divine Salamis, you will be responsible for the loss of children."

During this discordant period, Themistocles began expounding his opinion, refuting this point of view. His view was that if the gods meant that the Athenians would be destroyed at Salamis, they would not use the term "divine," but rather a word with a negative meaning. According to Themistocles, the term was a favorable sign for the Athenians and he supported the view that Athens should rely on its fleet and seek a naval engagement against the Persian forces.

Herodotus reports that the Athenians adopted Themistocles' views. Plutarch confirms this account, but temporally places the oracle a little before the naval battle at Salamis. Herodotus, on the other hand, places it before the Congress at Isthmus and he particularly mentions it twice: before the Congress at Isthmus and before the evacuation of Attica. As a result, questions arise concerning the actual date of the oracles. Do the oracles precede the facts or do they postdate them? Apart from that, another interpretation of the story is possible. Themistocles may have manipulated the oracles, along with other "signs" (for example, the disappearance of the holy snake of Erechtheus, known as the *Oikouros Ophis*, the home-protecting serpent), in order to achieve the city's evacuation and the confrontation of the Persian invasion with the power of the Athenian fleet. It is known that Themistocles insistently and repeatedly called for the creation of a powerful fleet that would make Athens ruler of the seas.

As a matter of fact, since 493 BC, Themistocles had conceived an ambitious plan of building Athens into a naval force. Herodotus remarks that he supported this plan after a large amount of money had been accumulated in the public fund, emanating from the mines of Laurion. Aristotle estimates this sum as 100 *talents*, or 600,000 *attic drachmas* (the *talent* and the *drachma* being ancient Greek monetary units). The Athenians initially intended to dedicate one tenth of the sum to the gods and then distribute the rest, but Themistocles discouraged them from this and suggested instead that they build 200 ships in order to use them against Athens' rival, Aegina. In the end, according to Herodotus, the fleet was built, but it was never used for its initial purpose. It should be noted that the number of 200 vessels reported by Herodotus is not consistent with some other historians' calculations. Herodotus probably uses the initial number of ships as planned by Themistocles although only 100 triremes were actually built.

Themistocles to a great extent managed to put his plan into effect despite obstacles raised by his political opponents. In 480 BC, Athens had 147 operational warships and 53 in reserve. The Athenians had, once and for all, turned to the sea and this fact benefited them in the long run, because they possessed a capable naval force that (if supplemented with more ships) would make them competitive against the Persians or, for that matter, any other enemy. In contrast, those Athenians who were apprehensive of accepting Themistocles' advice, and, rather than escape to Troezen, Salamis, and Aegina, built a wooden wall and took cover inside the Acropolis, were unfortunately, massacred by the Persians following Xerxes' occupation and sack of Athens.

The trireme

The warship of the two rival fleets during the naval Battle of Salamis

Many conflicts have been determined by technological differences between the two opponents, usually with the one possessing the more advanced weapons prevailing. In the case of Salamis, however, the two rivals had similar weapons and equipment, with the Persians slightly dominating. But, there were other reasons besides the marvelous warship – the trireme – for the Greek success.

The actual inventor of the trireme, as well as the precise moment of its creation, remain unknown. According to a generally accepted belief, ships of this type were first built in the nautically advanced country of Phoenicia, particularly in the city of Sidon (now Sayda, in southern Lebanon), and Phoenician seamen carried its use throughout the rest of the Mediterranean world. An extant sculpture confirms that the Phoenicians sailed biremes as early as the 8th Century BC, if not earlier. Consequently, the relative research had already begun there and the invention of the trireme followed as a logical subsequent link in the evolution of the technology.

According to Thucydides, in the Greek metropolitan world, which was, of course, in continuous communication with the East, the first person to manufacture triremes was the Corinthian Ameinocles from the great family of the Bacchiadae.

Construction appears to have taken place during the late 8th Century (likely in 705 BC), when Periander ruled over Corinth, and was considered to be one of the seven wisest Greeks of his time. A man of brilliance and foresight, Periander fully understood the importance of constructing a powerful warship, far superior to any previously used, for a state primarily dependent on maritime trade – as Corinth was in the 8th and 7th Centuries BC. Such a weapon would give its users technological precedence over actual or possible opponents.

More specifically, it appears that the invention of the trireme was the result of the need of the organized state of Corinth to beat off the pirates that preyed on maritime shipping routes and impeded the Corinthians' trade with their colonies. Sailing light, fast vessels, the pirates would overtake and attack the merchant freighters, and then quickly slip away with their plunder. In order to confront the marauders effectively, the Corinthians needed a ship faster than all existing ones and armed sufficiently to inflict considerable damage on an opponent. What was required was a vessel that would pit ship against ship, rather than crew against crew, as had been the case in naval operations up to that point.

The pentecounter, the prevailing warship at that time (8th Century BC), lacked the speed necessary for such a mission, because it was powered by a total of 50 oars, or sweeps, arranged in

The trireme

a single continuous row, 25 to each side. It would appear that the practice of arranging the sweeps in two rows, one above the other, arose in the coastal cities of Ionia; it was an invention possibly known to the Corinthian seamen. The ship that featured two layers of sweeps (with, consequently, corresponding places for the oarsmen) was called a bireme and had almost 100 sweeps, ensuring a higher speed than that of the penteconter. Later, Ameinocles dared to add a third line of oars, thus increasing the total to 150, and with the probable aim of further improving the sailing speed. The success of the design lies in the harmonious combination achieved from the ship's limited enlargement in length, height and width and the significant increase in motive power (from 50 oarsmen to 150 - 170).

The Corinthians launched a technological revolution with their new ship, the construction data of which they attempted to keep confidential. Their technical secret was revealed soon enough, however, as many people were able to observe and copy the new type of vessel. Construction and use of the trireme spread not only within the Greek world but also among the neighboring nations. The vessel took part in naval engagements where it proved an effective weapon. Throughout the 5th Century BC, it was the primary warship in the Aegean Sea and was also well known throughout the rest of the Mediterranean. In addition to the Phoenicians and Greeks, the Cilicians, the Carians, the Pamphylians, the Egyptians, and others put it to use.

During the Persian Wars, the Ionian rebels used predominantly

The reconstructed trireme *Olympias.*

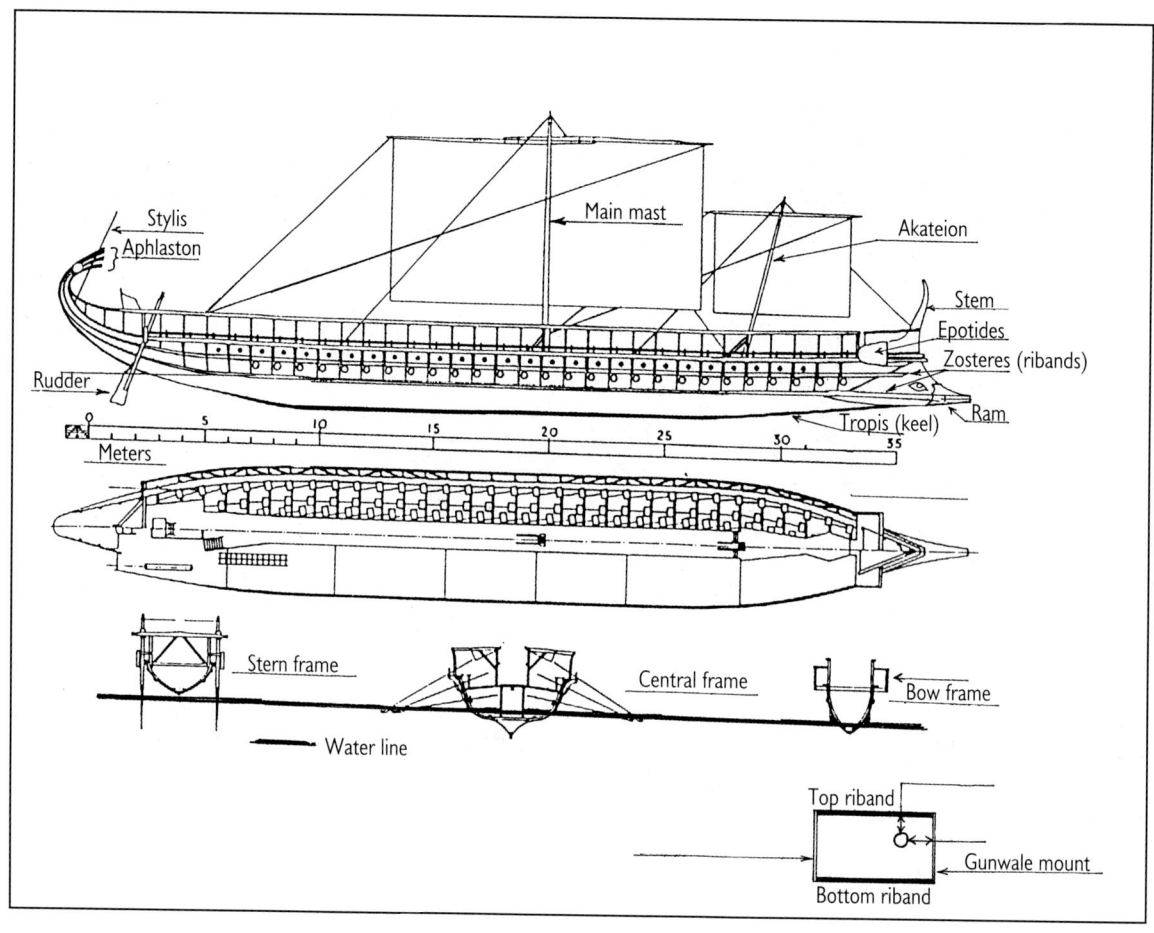

Starboard side illustration, ground plan and bow, stern, and middle cross sections of Olympias. *Top right: the graduated cubit used for making the oars (sweeps). Bottom right: diagram showing the position of the* thalamitae *oar apertures.*

triremes, as did their compatriots, the Greeks of the metropolitan country, during all the crucial naval confrontations (Lade, Artemisium, Salamis, Mycale, the Eurymedon River, etc.). The ships were not exactly the same as each other, however; there were many variants sporting different degrees of improvement. The warships that took part at the Battle of Salamis were of an early type, much simpler in construction, without even a deck or other unnecessary elements.

The trireme remained in use for over 400 years (from roughly 700 BC to 300 BC), and was eventually replaced by other, even larger ships (quadriremes, quinquiremes, etc.) that more successfully met the escalating requirements of naval warfare.

Representations – Reports

Unfortunately, no authentic trireme has been preserved (mainly because wood rots quickly), while even its representations – either paintings or engravings – are extremely rare, probably because of the difficulty of faithfully drawing the complicated construction. A few representations do exist, however, the most important of which is that of the famous Lenormant relief on the Acropolis (410 – 400 BC). There are also color representations on several unearthed contemporary pots, such as the representation of the stern on the Urn of Talos. The outline of a prow complete with a ram is represented on the sepulchral stele of Democleides in the Greek National

Archaeological Museum, while on that of Demetrius in the Glyptothek in Munich, the prow is represented again but in the opposite direction with a ram, *epotides* (beams projecting like ears on each side of a ship's bows), and an outrigger (*parexeiresia*, a wooden construction that was built out from the ship's sides and was occupied by the third row of oarsmen, the *thranitae*). Equally important, of course, for determining the various dimensions of these ships are the boat building sheds (*neosoikoi*) of the Piraeus at Zea (late 5th Century BC), which was one of the foremost naval stations of antiquity. Some of the ancient boat sheds were very recently discovered and measured underwater, giving an idea as to the maximum dimensions of the vessel.

Moreover, there are pertinent reports found in ancient literature (the works of Herodotus, Aeschylus, Thucydides, Diodorus Siculus, Plutarch, and others), in inscriptions, and various archival texts, including the archives of the boat sheds' commissaries. Another source of information is the completely preserved stele, describing the *skeuotheke* (arsenal) of the 4th-Century BC architect Philon of Eleusis. The *skeuotheke* was the large building at Athens' port, the Piraeus, in which the rigging and other equipment for Athens' warships were stored.

General characteristics of the ship

As is usually the case with warships, the trireme had a basic oblong shape. It was relatively light, of simple wood construction, was fast and low, and was fitted with a flat keel.

The majority of modern authors agree that the average trireme was 33 to 37 meters long (according to the prevailing version, though there are other estimates suggesting a length of 40 meters), 3.50 to 4.40 meters wide, and stood 2.1 to 2.5 meters above water (underwater it has been calculated that it drew around 1 meter). These estimates are based on the dimensions of the boat sheds that were built at the great naval station of Athens in Zea to protect the ships, as well as on the number of oarsmen (85 to each side), and on the length of the third rowing deck, the *parexeiresia*.

The ship consisted of a light hull that began with the keel, usually made of oak, a rigid timber, onto which the entire ship was constructed. Lighter wood (elm or plane) was used for the three *zosteres* (ribands or long planks of wood that were laid horizontally and constituted the ship's backbone) surrounding the keel. The *zosteres* were strengthened by the *hypozomata*, which were thick ropes used for lashing together and tightening the wooden parts of the ship. A wide variety of construction materials was employed, depending on the capability of the boat builder. In his *Enquiry into Plants*, Theophrastus, the ancient biologist and student of Aristotle, was very illuminating on the topic of ship construction: "The fir, therefore, the pine and the wild cypress are, generally speaking, very useful in shipbuilding, since the triremes and the warships are made of fir, because of its lightness, and the commercial ships of pine because it does not rot. Certain naval constructors, however, also build triremes of this (pine) because they do not find enough fir. In Syria and Phoenicia they use cedar, since they cannot get enough pine. In Cyprus, however, they use parasol, since this tree grows on the island and it seems to be better than their pine. Most parts are made of these kinds of wood.

Olympias **on her maiden voyage.**

However, the keel of the triremes is made of oak, so that it can sustain the ship's launch. Certain constructors make the "ribs" of the triremes out of parasol, because they are light ... , the cat-heads (straight pieces of wood) are made of ash tree wood, black mulberry and elm wood ..." (*Book 5.7.1-3*)

Across the ship, joists stuck out from the sides, two at the front and two at the rear, at the same height as the highest riband. The anchors hung from the forward ones, which were located at the prow and were called *epotides* (they were so called as they looked like ears sticking out from the ship), while the two rudders were fixed to the stern joists. In the area between these cross-joists and mounted on them along the ship, was the narrow wooden platform called the *parexeiresia* upon which the third, and biggest line of oarsmen, the *thranitae*, sat.

On the prow was a small, flat platform, an *ikrion*, that reached the edge of the ship and on which the observer-officer (*prorates*) stood. Tradition called for a decorative end on the wooden joist (in seamen's language, the "stem"), which was joined vertically with the other wooden joists that were placed horizontally and that ran through the entire ship. This part of the prow was named the *akrostolion* and it was combined with inlaid painted eyes on the side of the hull next to the prow. These eyes were painted in various colors and, in combination with the color of the rest of the prow; they created the impression of the ship with eyes looking forward. If we also take into account the *epotides*, which looked like ears, and the oars, that stuck out like wings, the entire ship was presented as a live marine creature.

On the stern were the rudders, which were, in fact, two thick oars with wide blades (quite similar to those on modern boats having a wooden manual rudder on the stern). There was one such oar on each side of the ship and they were linked to each other, the tiller or vertical handle of the rudder was called the *oiax*. The rudders were handled by a helmsman, called a commander, who stood on a small platform suitably shaped for this laborious work (another *ikrion*). The trireme's actual commander, the captain of the vessel, was known as the *trierarch*. The raised and decorated end of the stern was called the *aphlaston*, and differed from ship to ship. Just forward of the center section was a mast, called *stylis*, which sometimes carried a flag, sometimes a plate with the ship's name and also sometimes the emblem of a particular deity. This plate usually distinguished the ships of the various states, in case there was no other distinctive mark, such as placing the shields along the *parexeiresia* or a flag on the main mast.

The trireme

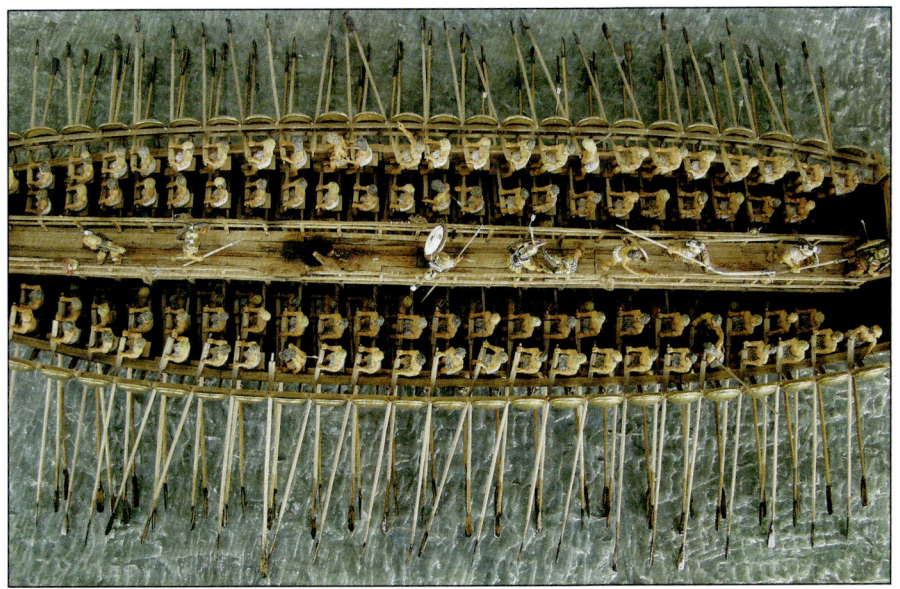

Overhead view of a trireme model. (Scratch built model in 1:72 scale by Stamatis Papanikolaou, photo by Stelios Demiras/ "Model Expert" magazine, Periscopio Publications)

Shipbuilding

In powerful Athens, the shipbuilder (*architect*) was chosen from among the many experts who showed up for the job. It is not certain that he really was a shipbuilder, in the sense of having special knowledge, but was rather a contractor or (in modern terms) a project manager, who organized the entire shipbuilding operation, having his own group of experts (shipbuilders, carpenters, etc.,) and workers. Some contractors were possibly related either directly or indirectly to the timber trade.

All the work was done in a simple shipyard, sited on a suitable beach, with the timber rammed into the sand. Tools were definitely used, probably wooden ones (e.g. graduated rules used for counting), as are employed in small shipyards even today. The shipbuilding techniques and the relevant knowledge were passed down by the older craftsmen to the young workers, and also within families, in keeping with the tradition for a young man to follow in his father's footsteps.

The ships were all built in the same manner, as far as most of the basics were concerned. This also helped with the economics of the whole enterprise, since a high degree of standardization of manufactured goods allows for a great economy of scale and, consequently, lower production costs and a greater profit margin. Obviously, the commissioning agent always ordered an adequate number of ships, not just a few units, while sometimes (in case of war) the pace of the construction played a decisive role. At the time of the Peloponnesian War, when Callicratidas besieged the Athenian force of Conon in Mytilene, a new fleet of 110 new triremes was very rapidly built in the shipyards of Attica, which hurried to fight and defeat the Spartans at Arginouses (405 BC).

The shipbuilder was only allowed to improvise on the ram and on the exterior decoration. The latter usually was up to the ship's supreme officer to decide, that is to say, the trierarch for Athens, whenever, of course, there was time and money for such a thing. The shipbuilder, however, was allowed to write his name on a special part of the ship.

Where the aforementioned shipyards were located still remains a mystery. It is unknown whether Athens, which was the greatest commissioning agent and user of triremes in the Greek world during the 4th and 5th Centuries BC, had its own shipyards somewhere in Attica or elsewhere in the Aegean, possibly in Thrace or in another area close to the raw materials required for their construction. It is also not known whether the contractors were Athenian citizens or of other citizenship (such as the resident aliens known as *Metics*), and it is therefore not entirely clear whether the particular shipbuilding tradition was an inspiration of Athenian families or a mixture of many traditions. Whatever the case, it is known that, since the time of the Battle of Salamis the various Asiatic shipyards could build taller, faster, and more richly decorated ships that sailed well on the open sea. This superiority appears to have disappeared later, due to development and improvements made on the Athenian ships. Nevertheless, the precise location of the building sites of those excellent ships remains a mystery.

The Deck

In its initial form, the trireme was very simple and had no continuous deck, in the sense of a single level. On the contrary, it was laid out like a large boat. Also, there were no handrails, probably in order to facilitate boarding and disembarkation. The boat was open, apart from the two platforms (*ikria*) on the bow and stern, and two corridors on either side connecting these platforms that were built on top of the *parexeiresia*, leaving space for those not rowing. This situation created a number of problems, the foremost of which was the permanent exposure of the entire crew (especially the oarsmen) not only to the weather, but also to the missiles of any potential enemy. One way to combat this situation was to use shields fixed to the sides of the ship, at the height of the *parexeiresia*. The ships that covered themselves with such glory at Salamis in September 480 BC were of this type.

Following the naval operations caused by the Persian invasion of Greece, and according to the design of the Phoenician ships, the triremes were built with a single deck that linked the two sides on the *parexeiresia*. Those triremes were called "covered" or *cataphract* and were, of course, more powerful than the earlier models. Here it should be made clear that the name *cataphract* did not mean "armored" ship, as it had no iron plates. This name was derived from the fact that their total wooden construction was stronger compared to all known predecessors.

In the *cataphract* triremes, the existence of the deck allowed easy movement, and afforded the crew more comfort. It also had an important disadvantage, however: it increased the total weight of the vessel. The *cataphract* triremes weighed 45, and even 50 tons and that resulted in a proportional reduction in speed and maneuverability. These modifications seem to have been brought about by Kimon during his expeditions along the coastline of Ionia (the Battle of the Eurymedon River, etc.) some 14 years after Salamis, and are why the Athenian triremes, from that time, evolved their own design.

There is little doubt that the Greek triremes that fought at Salamis were still the early type, that is, without a deck. Precisely because of this, they were much lower in the water and more stable. In contrast, the Asiatic ships that took part in the battle appear to have been triremes of a

The trireme

Three-quarter view of the trireme model from the stern. (Scratch built model in 1:72 scale by Stamatis Papanikolaou, photo by Stelios Demiras / "Model Expert" magazine, Periscopio Publications)

more advanced type, with a single-piece deck and higher prows and sterns. In consequence they were higher, more unstable, and more vulnerable to weather changes.

Propulsion

The triremes were designed to be driven either by the force of the winds or the strength of the oarsmen (*eiresia*), or even a combination of both.

In the combat conditions for which the warship was constructed, the trireme was primarily driven by oarsmen. Aristotle characterized triremes as "rowing machines." Nowadays, scholars are in general agreement that the ship was designed in such a way as to take advantage of the combined strength of a large number of men, many more, in fact, than what its length allowed (170 oars instead of 54). This was achieved by the appropriate arrangement of the oarsmen on three levels, very close to each other (especially on the two lower levels) but slightly apart. The oarsmen on the lower level (*thalamitae*) sat immediately over the keel in the hold, that is, the deep internal space of the ship. The oarsmen on the next level (*zygitae*) sat a little higher, at the height of the lower-level oarsmen's shoulders. The *zygitae* were positioned next to the *zyga*, the transverse girders of the ship, hence their name. Finally, the oarsmen on the third level, the *thranitae*, were located in that part of the ship that stuck out over the sides and was called *parexeiresia*, almost at the height of the shoulders of the *zygitae*. As the converging form of the ship did not cut down on their number, there were more of these than on the two lower rows (62 instead of 54). It is certain that there was just one rower to each oar. These three successive lines of oars (and oarsmen handling them) gave the boat its characteristic name: *trireme*.

As a warship, it was essential that the trireme be able to execute careful and highly controlled maneuvers. Oars provided greater control and safety than wind power in fulfilling such a function. The oars differed depending on the position of the oarsmen manning them, but according to historically accepted theory, they were all of the same length (4.2 to 4.4 meters). The differences between them

An impressive view of the epibatae onboard the trireme under fire from a rain of Persian arrows and spears. (Scratch built model in 1:72 scale by Stamatis Papanikolaou, photo by Stelios Demiras / "Model Expert" magazine, Periscopio Publications)

lay in the shapes of the actual oar or sweep blade, on the basis of the different angles at which the different tiers of oars hit the surface of the water. Oars of the first line (that of the *thalamitae*) entered the water at a much smaller angle as they were very close to the actual water level and, so, these had an oblong blade, while the oars of the *thranitae* had an almost a rectangular blade.

When under way but not in combat, the ship could use its sails. It actually had two sails made of linen fabric, a large one (the "great sail") and a smaller one (the *akateion*), although, in fact, they were never used simultaneously, but rather alternately. For long voyages, the great sail, which hung from the ship's main mast, was hoisted. This sail was of considerable height and width, but if caught by the strong wind, made the ship hard to steer (due to the inefficient steering arrangement and especially the vessel's low, broad keel). If the ship was about to engage in a battle, this sail was furled, taken down, and left on any convenient (that is to say, near and friendly) landfall. During operations, the smaller sail, the *akateion*, was used (which made the ship easier to handle). It was hoisted on its own mast forward of the main mast, and used in combination with the oars.

Armament – Ram

The trireme, having been designed for military use, was built to carry special elements of armament. The most important was the ram or *embolon*, namely a metal or wooden protrusion (up to 2 meters long) of the two lower *zosteres* (ribands) giving the impression that it was the continuation of the keel (while it actually was separate). It was fixed horizontally and at right angles to the stem (the length of wood that stood vertically at the prow). The ram was most commonly built of wood and sheathed in metal, which increased strength and power. The weight of such a ram could reach 200 kilos. Sometimes, in addition to the primary ram but somewhat higher, there was another, smaller one that was fixed at the height of the third (highest) riband. The primary ram had two or three "teeth" and was usually made in the form of an animal or marine monster.

The trireme

The addition of a ram was no longer an innovative idea; it had been known from much earlier times. The pentaconters had been fitted with a ram as were the biremes. It appears, however, that they were rarely used as an assault weapon, perhaps because large-scale naval battles were also very rare events. According to Herodotus, the ram was used as an offensive weapon for the first time in a naval operation in 540 BC during the important naval Battle of Alalia (off Corsica) between the Greek settlers, originally from Phocaea in Ionia, and the Carthaginians and their Tyrrhenian allies who wanted to expel them. The Greeks prevailed, although with many losses, while all their ships that were saved had their rams twisted, a fact that probably indicates the overall weakness of the new type of weapon. Whatever the case, it has never been established whether the ships that took part in that battle were triremes; most likely they were not. In another report Herodotus offers the information that, in 525 BC, the tyrant of Samos, Polycrates, had definitely built a fleet of triremes. Other writers, including Hipponax of Ephessus, also mention the use of triremes equipped with rams at that time, and, thus, it would appear that the use of the new ship design was widespread by the late 6th Century BC.

The trireme and the ram are so interconnected that it is impossible to determine whether the ship was designed in order to render possible the effective use of the ram or the other way around, that is to say, whether the ram was added to the new ship in order to give the vessel a greater assault capability. The answer to this question is irrelevant, however, as the two elements were harmoniously combined into an organic whole. The trireme was commanded and entered battle in such a way that it could make good use of its main offensive weapon, the ram.

All the great naval battles of the first half of the 5th Century (Lade, Artemisium, Salamis, Eurymedon, etc.) were undertaken following tactics that sought to utilize the most efficient use of the ram. With these tactics, the Athenian navy gained the reputation of being very capable, establishing its fame and a successful method of action.

This method consisted of maneuvering around the enemy vessel until the attacker could get into the most suitable angle to ram (never full on the bow or stern), and then it attacked at full speed. The aim was to ram the hostile ship in such a way so that it would bend and finally capsize. Such an outcome was, however, rather uncommon and it definitely required the skill of a very capable captain. In the majority of cases, the attacking ship stuck its ram into the opponent's hull. This resulted in the other ship filling with water and sinking. Immediately after striking the enemy,

A view of the trireme's stern where the helmsman's seat can clearly be seen. (Scratch built model in 1:72 scale by Stamatis Papanikolaou, photo by Stelios Demiras / "Model Expert" magazine, Periscopio Publications)

however, the attacker had to withdraw its ram quickly and back away to prevent being pulled under by the resulting maelstrom created by the sinking ship. At this juncture, it should be mentioned that the ship could also move in reverse, with the appropriate movements of the oarsmen.

As expected, during the following years (second half of the 5th Century BC) a number of design modifications were attempted by different opponents of the Athenians to enable them to compete against them successfully. Since the Athenians were unbeatable in all the known methods of action, a number of antidotes were tried, but were ultimately unsuccessful.

Thucydides quite vividly recounts the thinking of the Syracusians during their participation in the Peloponnesian War: "They had arranged the rest of their navy in such the way that they had observed from the previous naval battle, which could give them an advantage over the enemy (namely the Athenians and their allies, who had invaded Sicily and besieged the Syracusians in 415 BC). To be more specific, they removed the ships' prows in order to make them shorter and more solid. They adapted thick *epotides* on the prows and supported them from below with abutments six cubits long up to the inside and outside sidewall of the ship. They followed precisely the same way with which the Corinthians repaired their ships and strengthened them in the prows, when they fought against the Athenians in Naupaktos (in 429 BC during the first period of the Peloponnesian War). This was because the Syracusians believed that they would thus hold a major advantage over the Athenians' ships, as they were not built in the same way. On the contrary, theirs had thin prows, because they did not use to strike the enemy ships in the prow, but rather in the sides with their rams (an already known method of the Athenians), after previously having circled around the enemy ship."
(*Bk 7, ch. 21, Peloponnesian Wars*)

Crew and administration

The extant ancient sources – Herodotus, Thucydides, Demosthenes, etc., – all agree that 200 men were required to crew a trireme, excluding the commander, the trierarch, who was in overall command of the ship and, in Athens' case, was also paid the expenses for its maintenance. Of those 200 men, 16 were deck crew (sailors), 14 were the military force attached to each boat (the *epibatae* or "marines"), while the remaining 170 were the oarsmen (*eretae*).

More specifically, the following were included in the 16 deck crew: the captain-helmsman of the ship (who was also called *captain*, *archos*, *naukleros*, or *oiakostrophos*, because it was he who handled the two rudders); another officer who stood on the prow (with the role of principal lookout) and was called *prorates*; a third officer (the *keleustes* petty officer) who directed the oarsmen; a fourth officer whose title survived from the previous age of the pentecontarchos (in earlier times he was in charge of the crew, but in the trireme he undertook the role of a modern secretary, namely the ship's paymaster); a fifth officer (called *naupegos*, that is "shipwright") who specialized in technical matters and was in charge of all the ship's repairs and maintenance, etc.; a musician (called *auletes* or *trieraules*) who was responsible for the rowing rhythm; and finally 10 able seamen who

The trireme

The one surviving side view of a trireme. (5th Century BC relief, Acropolis Museum, Athens)

handled the sails and the rest of the day-to-day running of the ship.

The 14 *epibatae* (marines) attached to the ship to protect it consisted of 10 soldiers and four archers. The former were citizens of the middle social classes who stood alongside their equals to form the *phalanx* during land operations. Onboard ship, because of their social status, they were looked upon as officers and, hierarchically, were immediately under the *trierarch*. In the event of action, they fought on the deck, with their mission being to protect the ship from any enemy assault. In the same way, the four archers formed a protective screen around the captain who handled the rudders and, consequently, were positioned with him on the stern. The number of the *epibatae* was later increased and could even reach 40 men. During Xerxes' expedition, the Persian ships had been reinforced with more soldiers, 30 in total, who served as guards for their vessels and fought aboard ship during the battles.

Depending on the position in which they were seated on the three different levels of the trireme, the 170 oarsmen (or *eretae*) were divided into the 54 *thalamitae* who sat at the lowest level, the 54 *zygitae* who sat on the level above the *thalamitae* but in such a way that a *zygotes* would be located between two *thalamitae*. The *thalamitae*, as well as the *zygitae*, sat on continuous benches, called *thranio*, which were located inside the ship's hull.

Finally, the 62 *thranitae* sat in specially allocated positions on the highest level, in the space created by the *parexeiresia*. The *thranitae*, in contrast to the *zygitae* and the *thalamitae*, sat high on the ship's sides and not inside the ship; as a result, they could see the sea around them but were also more vulnerable to missile attacks (javelins, arrows, stones, etc.).

The crucial role played by the oarsmen was generally recognized. The existence of three different levels upon which they were arranged, the way they mustered and their coordination, particularly during the battles when difficult and fast maneuvers were necessary, made theirs a demanding career. It meant that they required continuous training to enable them to act effectively in unison, something that only the organized naval forces of powerful cities (such as Athens, Corinth, and Syracuse) could ensure.

The great modern scholar of the trireme, Emmanouel Nellopoulos, wishing to elevate the oarsmen's role, writes quite emphatically, ". . . This human machine was called *eretikon*. It owed its speed mainly to the oarsmen. However, these oarsmen had to handle the oar (*eretmon*) skillfully,

Model of an Athenian trireme from the 5th Century BC, although not quite accurate: the ship appears to have a normal through-deck, which was not the case at the time of the Battle of Salamis and, moreover, the stern appears to be elevated suggesting some sort of posterior construction. (Maritime Museum of Piraeus)

jointly, and rhythmically as a human being, in various rhythms and waves of the sea, each time reaching the necessary speed up to the highest possible point... In order, therefore, to achieve this as well as innumerable other details, having the ideal order and discipline as fundamental principles, not only the oarsmen had to try really hard, but also their leaders, particularly the petty officer, who acted like a tireless and unbending watchdog, and his assistants, the two *toicharchoi*. Unaffected by the emotions of the battle or by the sea's lurching, rowing and not fighting, rowing and being hit, tired and hurt, out of breath, dizzy in the sultry atmosphere of the hull, restless, contorted in their narrow space, hungry, thirsty and despite all this executing, with persistence and admirable precision, the various and repeated orders of the intelligent, dynamic and indomitable petty officer, they maneuvered like dolphins, circumnavigating and breaking through they rammed and tacked in defiance of death by drowning as well!"

It should be noted, that the oarsmen of the Greek triremes were neither slaves nor convicts but free citizens who undertook precisely this profession, that of oarsmen. Many authors, when writing about Athens, refer to it as the "democracy of the seamen" or the oarsmen. Of course, in extraordinary instances slaves were recruited as oarsmen, just as they were also used in land operations. Sometimes this eventually led to their emancipation, as a proof of the appreciation of their labor aboard ship. There were also cases of compulsory service of slaves, although in a lower percentage compared to that of the free oarsmen. Something similar was likely to happen in less powerful cities, both demographically and economically, due to the lack of professional oarsmen. Finally, it should be noted that the triremes were never used as prisons or hellish torture for those serving on board – in consequence, the apertures for the oars were not closed off so as to prevent the oarsmen from escaping into the sea, as was the case with the Roman triremes a few centuries later.

Anchor

Even though several archaic anchors have been discovered and preserved, the precise shape of the trireme's anchor has yet to be ascertained. At the naval station of Zea, below sea level, there exist many stone structures in the form of truncated pyramids with a horizontal

The trireme

aperture through the sides and a metal ring on the top. Most probably they were stable anchors, to which the boats moored.

It is also certain that the ship carried its own anchor(s), albeit of unknown shape, probably made of metal (probably iron, since copper, being much lighter, would have been unsuitable), or even wood with a stone counterbalance. It is also known from several naval inscriptions that its weight reached 45 *mnas*, namely 19.647 kilograms. This low weight leads to the reliable conclusion that the ship did not rely on the anchor for its safe moorage. From all the existing sources, it can be concluded that the trireme was a ship made to be hauled up onto the beach, and not to lie at anchor in the open sea. The stern's elevated construction implies that the ship was hauled from there and, consequently, the anchor, which hung from the prow, merely supplemented the ship's secure mooring on land.

Appearance – Color

From existing contemporary sources, it can be concluded that the ships were painted with a red lead paint (a suitable color for maintenance) to make them waterproof and, obviously, reddish. Since the time of the Persian Wars, however, records exist that refer to triremes painted, at least on the prow, in either a black or dark blue color.

Military role

The primary role of the trireme was as a warship. The vessel was an instrument of battle and was built to be able to oppose any hostile naval units, either individually or participating *en masse* in a naval battle, and it had to deal with them successfully.

Its military role was specialized into the many ways that corresponded to different missions. The simplest of these was to patrol the coasts of the country and outlying islands (Attica, Samos, Chios, etc.), protecting the shore from hostile raids. The opposite also happened of course: the trireme often functioned as a raiding ship against coastal regions of other states. In this case, the soldiers landed when the ship entered shallow gulfs and sailed almost up onto the shore. The very low draught (1 meter) and the solid construction allowed the ship almost to run aground, landing the epibatae very close to the beach. In case of a raid on the hostile port, the situation became easier as the soldiers could land directly on the jetties or piers. A mention should, perhaps, be made concerning the raid on the harbor of Piraeus itself by the

Side view of a trireme. (Illustration by Demetrios Hadoulas)

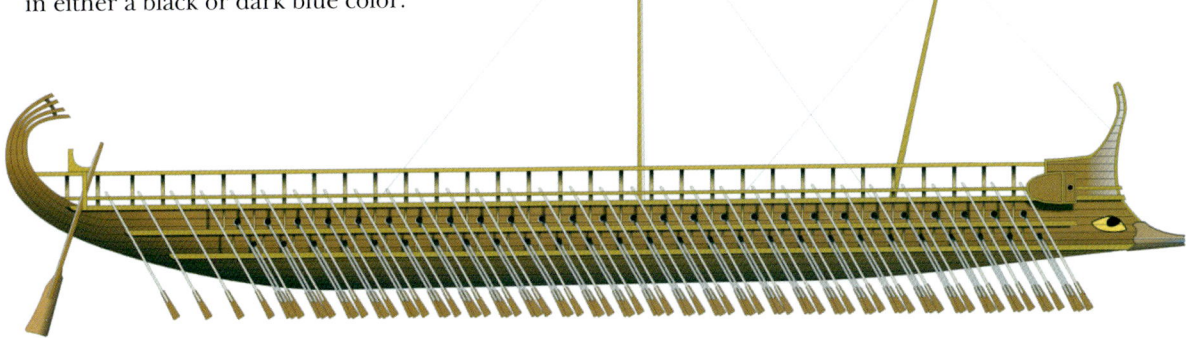

The reconstructed trireme Olympias. *Note the* askomata *(animal skins) seals and the ropes with which they were tied to the oars. This technique prevented seawater from entering the ship.*

Lacedaemonians and the Aeginians under the commands of the skillful Aeginian admiral, Teleutias, in the summer of 387 BC.

The trireme was primarily designed to participate in naval battles in conjunction with other ships of its kind (preferably near coasts and not in the open sea), rather than carry out patrols and naval raids. In the case of naval battles it clearly revealed its special characteristics, both positive and negative.

The advantages were:

● On the whole, the light construction (its weight reached just 45 tons fully loaded) allowed easy handling under all conditions: from its hauling up on the beach, which was particularly useful due to the need for frequent mooring and the limited number of friendly harbors, up to its very rapid launching, in order to get up to speed quickly at sea, ready to face the enemy or any other threat.

● Its significant speed, which came from the combination of light construction, shallow keel, and the increased motive power compared to all earlier ship types. With just its sails set, it could reach a speed up to 5 knots. Using just the oarsmen's strength, the speed could be as high as around 8 knots, while a combination of both would give the ship anything up to 10 knots.

● Its maneuverability, which was the result of both the earlier-mentioned advantages and its moderate size, particularly as far as its length restriction of less than 35 meters was concerned. Indeed, it could be looked at as an oblong ship.

● Georgios Steinhauer also adds a fourth advantage, the validity of which, however, is seriously disputed: "Because of its light construction, the trireme could be smashed but it could not sink. Despite the frequently used word "submerge," this is obvious in the records concerning the crew's fate and the remains of the rammed triremes, but also in the absence of trireme shipwrecks. Thus is also explained the trierarch's obligation to rescue and deliver the ram of the destroyed trireme."

Apart from the advantages, the trireme also had ample disadvantages. Steinhauer records them:

"...It was not a safe ship: it was shallow and could not withstand a storm and, moreover, it required frequent repairs because of its off-hand construction; this constituted a serious disadvantage during naval operations. This lack of endurance in bad weather conditions compelled the trireme not to venture far from the coasts very often, with all the dangers (for example a shipwreck) and the restrictions that this involved for the tactics and strategy of naval warfare. Actually, the trireme faced considerable problems as far as carrying out regular movements was concerned. Thus, for example, the instability, due to the ship's low draught, constituted a serious weakness in performing maneuvers in strong winds, as the naval battles of Patras and Arginouses proved.

On the other hand, the use of the

trireme as a strategic weapon also appears problematic, due to the weakness in accomplishing basic strategic objectives. These included the effective blockade of the enemy from the sea (due to the ship's limited endurance in bad weather conditions) and the realization of distant expeditions. Transporting an adequate number of soldiers (marines) and the necessary supplies for a long journey was, indeed, impossible due to the lack of usable storage space and the great number of oarsmen. Moreover, the ship depended on many bases or friendly markets for its supply and overnight stay; it also depended on safe and more permanent bases for its maintenance and mooring during the period of the year when navigation was impossible. The destruction of the Athenian fleet in the harbor of Syracuse was due precisely to the lack of regular maintenance (caulking etc.) of the ships... The financial disadvantages of the trireme should also be added to the above strategic ones, which also had serious repercussions on the strategy of naval warfare. These were the requirements in raw materials (timber, particularly long timber for the keel and mast, and tar) that had to be imported, apart from the enormous expenses both in money for their construction and catering, and in personnel (a fleet of 200 triremes needed 34,000 oarsmen). The problems became greater if one took into consideration the rhythm of the fleet's constant replacement. This did not depend only on natural disasters or naval battles. A basic disadvantage of the trireme was its relatively short life span, due to its rough construction and abuse, particularly the frequent dragging up the beach and re-launching that, in turn, was due to the lack of its ability to moor offshore. From the dockyard commissaries' inscriptions, it can be concluded that the lifespan of a trireme was roughly around 20 years. This, however, called for regular and constant maintenance. If this did not happen, the triremes leaked and started to let in water, as often happened during extended expeditions. Thus, from several inscriptions, it can be surmised that the same trireme within three years of use was already characterized as "old."

Tactics during a naval battle

The trireme's fundamental aim was to ram the rival ship, and the usual tactic was the *diekplous* (to "break through and ram"), in essence, to penetrate the enemy fleet's formation and to get into a position suitable for ramming the sides of the opponent, either against its prow or against its stern, never in the center because this faced the risk of destroying the ram or even penetrating the enemy ship to such an extent (especially if the other ship was old or badly maintained with worn out sidewalls) that the attacker could become entrapped as well.

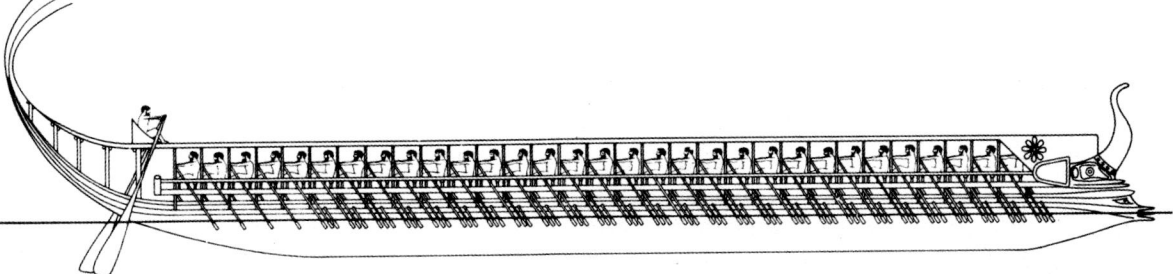

Side view of a trireme. This drawing is based on one found on a relief at the Acropolis. (Greek Military History)

According to modern estimates, the necessary speed for a successful ramming was up to 4 knots against the prow of the hostile ship (which was also moving forward) and 8 knots against its stern (which meant that the oarsmen had to row with all their strength). As Konstantinos Rados described in detail in his excellent book: "with the most maneuverable and best-sailing trireme, we have the introduction of the sudden penetration of the hostile array, of the turn in order to come next to the ship that has been selected and, finally, the attack against the enemy: What in the Greek navy is called *diekplous*" (break through and ram). Rados also explained the required conditions for the realization of this famous tactic in contrast to the tactics of larger, more sea-worthy vessels: "The implementation of this tactic presupposed a lot of space, the open sea. The tactic of the triremes, which were heavier and less maneuverable, was completely the opposite. They looked for straits, coves and narrow bays, where the lack of space prevented the enemy from gaining the most from his agility, speed, and great turning abilities..."

Another common tactic was that of circumnavigation – sailing around the enemy fleet's formation – until it was forced to retreat to such an extent that they crashed into each other or lost their battle order and thus became vulnerable. The essential condition for performing the circumnavigation maneuver was, without doubt, the existence of sufficient sea room as well as numerical supremacy of the fleet attempting it. In such a case, the fleet that was outnumbered, in order to avoid being surrounded, would attempt to seek shelter close to the coast where one, or even better, both sides were protected.

Both of the aforesaid tactics demanded naval mastery and ability on behalf of the captain as well as the oarsmen. Applying other tactics, as the Syracusians did with the *epotides*, did not require such a high degree of naval skill (this being why they were castigated at the time) but simply more powerful ships. Nevertheless, they showed that they had gained ground and very quickly, already by the late

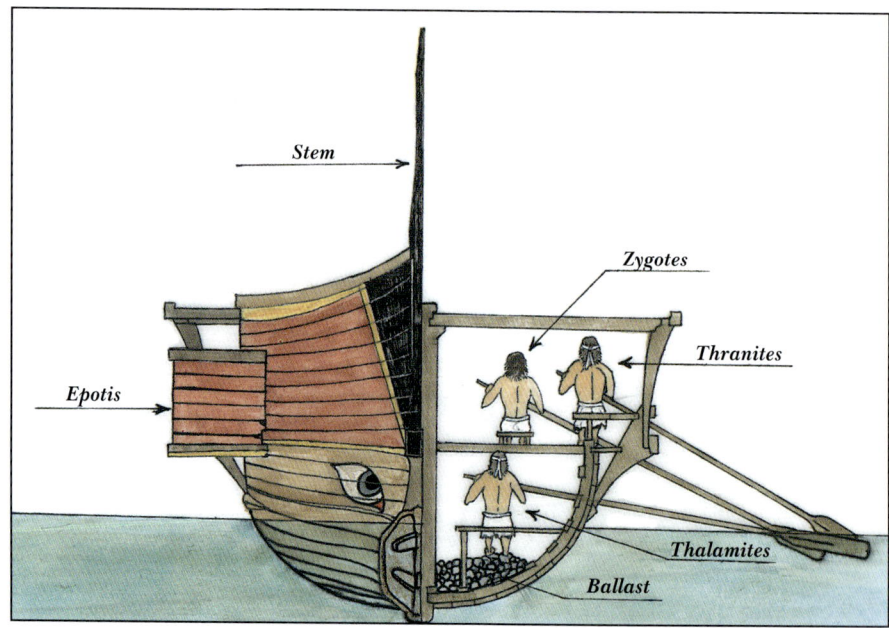

A sectional view of the prow of a trireme, where the arrangement of the three rows of oarsmen can be clearly seen. (Illustration by Stamatis Papanikolau)

The trireme

4th Century BC, triremes were beginning to be gradually replaced by new, larger, and more powerful ships (quadriremes, quinquiremes, etc.). The swansong of the trireme appears to have been the naval Battle of Amorgos in 322 BC, during which 240 Athenian triremes were defeated by the bigger ships of the Macedonians.

Modern times

A few years ago (in the 1980s) the Greek navy constructed a replica of a trireme that was christened *Olympias*. The drawings for the boat were based on the studies of the British scholars John F. Coates and John S. Morrison, the authenticity of certain basic calculations of which were, however, greatly disputed by other scholars, mainly Greek, including Emmanouel Nellopoulos and E. Tzachos. The process of construction as well as the actual operation of the ship (finally launched on 23 July 1987) raised many questions; at the same time, however, they answered many of the older ones. One important difference of opinion centered on the length of the ship. The writers disagreed on the measurement system used, with some scholars basing their calculations on the system used in the classical period while others referenced the system of later, Hellenistic times. Finally, the ship was built with a draught of 1.3 meters and length of 37 meters (that is, using a calculation, taking the cubit mentioned in ancient texts to equal 0.444 meter). The vessel, as constructed, however, could never sail faster than 7 knots, something that some people, including Tzachos, believe is due to the ship having an inadequate length. According to such scholars, the cubit should have been calculated as equaling 0.4913 meters, which would have given an overall ship length of 40 meters. Whatever the merits of both views, today *Olympias* is used in exceptional ceremonial circumstances, for example to transport the Olympic flame to Piraeus for the Olympic Games in August 2004, while its anchorage is located in the southern end of Phaleron Bay (Trocadero Park), which is where the pursued Persian ships headed following their defeat at Salamis.

Critique

As with all successful, relevant constructions, the trireme constituted a balanced blend of different characteristics. In particular, as Konstantinos Rados most masterfully observed, during the Battle of Salamis the Greek warship was a "rowing ship of the trireme type, oblong, thin, with beautiful figureheads. The upper parts (namely the section above the surface of the sea) hardly reached 2 meters in height. Its draught was almost 1 meter and its weight was roughly 50 tons. Its length was maximum 35 meters [It is now believed that the ship could reach up to 40 meters in length. – Author's note.], while its greatest width did not exceed four meters."

Side view of a trireme's prow. The epibatae *onboard are under a rain of Persian arrows and spears, while, at the same time, they are launching their own missiles. Although this is a Greek trireme, certain elements of its construction (i.e. its elevated prow), refer rather to an Ionian trireme of the Persian fleet. (Scratch built model in 1:72 scale by Stamatis Papanikolaou, photo by Stelios Demiras/ "Model Expert" magazine, Periscopio Publications)*

Themistocles
Victory's guide

The land of Attica bred some of the most important political leaders of ancient Greece whose lives embellished the historical course of its glorious capital, Athens. Among them was Themistocles who, though of humble origin, managed to ascend to the top of the political pedestal and lead Athens and the allied cities through the successful expedition at Salamis. His foremost enemy was actually himself and the negative elements of his character that rendered him unpleasant to his fellow-citizens and which finally forced him into exile, where he died.

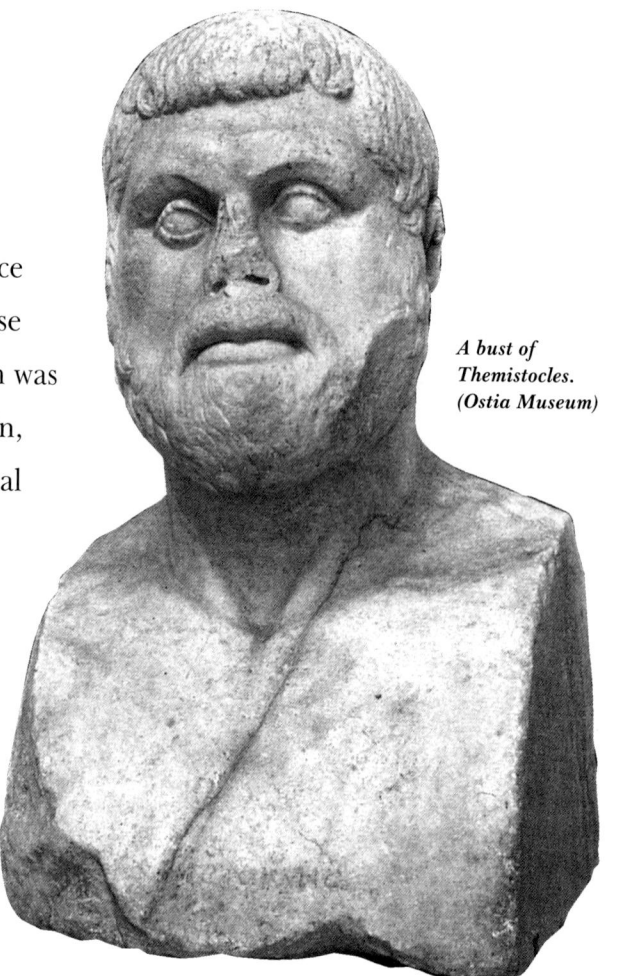

A bust of Themistocles. (Ostia Museum)

Themistocles was born one or two years after the death of Peisistratus, estimated to be around 525 or 526 BC, the son of Neocles who was related to the priestly and high-born Lycomedes family. Neocles resided in the municipality of Phrearrhioi and was a member of the Leontis tribe. His wife Euterpe, however, was of Carian origin probably from Halicarnassus. For this reason, the young Themistocles was not considered to be a legitimate Athenian citizen and so studied at the high school of Kynosarges, with other illegitimate Athenian offspring. The difficulties that he faced due to his origin were overcome thanks to the democratic reforms of Cleisthenes, who, in 508 BC, granted Athenian citizenship to all free male residents of the city.

Before Cleisthenes' favorable regulations, during his childhood, Themistocles convinced some young members of Athenian families to exercise with him at Kynosarges. Being restless and brilliant, he managed to distinguish himself among his peers for the intelligence and accuracy of his answers, at least in those courses that he believed contributed to the refinement of his character; he was unremarkable in the

Because of his humble background, Themistocles attended Kynosarges School that later roused the interest of many wealthy citizens. This is a wrestling scene in a gymnasium, as depicted on an ancient vase.

rest. In particular, when one of his schoolmates pointed out to him his weakness in music, Themistocles admitted that he was incapable of tuning his lyre and chanting, but was especially capable of increasing a city's power. His continuous study of orations prompted one of his teachers to tell him, rather prophetically, that he would not grow up to become something humble, but someone of stature and distinguished, either for good or evil.

Themistocles was also known for his avarice and a tendency to stand out among his fellow-citizens in both negative and positive ways. Plutarch reported that when he was young and unknown, he had invited Epicles, a musician from Hermione whom the Athenians particularly appreciated, to give lessons at his house. He also reported that when Themistocles was in Olympia attending the Olympic Games, he competed with Kimon in the opulence of his meals and accommodation, something that particularly annoyed the Athenians, as Kimon was of noble origin and such actions were totally acceptable for an individual of his class, but not for Themistocles who came from more humble background.

The first steps in the political setting

Themistocles had expressed his political interest very early, even though his father had tried to discourage him by constantly reminding him of the abandoned triremes on the beach, suggesting that the Athenians treated the once glorious, but later forgotten politicians in this way. Young Themistocles, however, attended almost any meeting of the *Ecclesia* (Athenian Assembly), and it is said that he knew the names of all his fellow-citizens, which flattered them and increased his popularity. His political career began in 493 BC, when he was elected an archon. From this position, believing that the Persians still remained a threat, he prompted the poet Phrynichus to present his play *The Fall of Miletus,* in order to remind the Athenian citizens of the recent tragic loss of Athens' colony, Miletus, to the Persians. For putting on the play, however, Phrynichus was punished with a fine of 1,000 Attic drachmas on the grounds that he had reminded Athenians of "familiar unpleasant things."

In 490 BC, when the Persian expedition began from the Cyclades and Euboea, Themistocles became a general and participated in the Battle of Marathon along with Aristeides, the leader of the aristocratic party. It is indeed said that he was so impressed by Miltiades' victory that he did not hesitate to admit that he had lost sleep thinking of his trophy. In one of the *Ecclesia* meetings Themistocles claimed that Athens was in a weak situation, and that it could only recover by creating a powerful fleet and a harbor. As soon as he had convinced his fellow-citizens of the validity of his words, he proposed to organize and fortify the harbor of Piraeus instead of the harbor of Phaleron, which had been used until then and, although Miltiades himself put forward objections, his proposal was finally accepted. Themistocles believed that the Persian king would not be discouraged by his defeat at Marathon and would, once again, attempt to invade Greece. The political disagreement between Themistocles and Aristeides focused on this point. The mutual resentment between the two men simmered for many years and, although at first it had no political fall-out, this changed in 489 BC, when Aristeides was elected an archon - judge. While Aristeides agreed with Themistocles that the Persian threat had not been averted, he believed that the Persian army would, once again, come overland. Consequently, he believed that the preparations of the Athenian navy were useless and, at the same time, he thought that the increase of the number of seamen and the power this could yield might upset the social scale of Athens. Their opposing views reached such a level of intensity that Aristeides proposed to the Athenians that they throw himself and Themistocles off a cliff in order to save themselves from their rivalry.

After Miltiades' death, very few politicians of note had remained in Athens. Among them were Aristeides and also Xanthippos, Pericles' father. Themistocles soon managed to eliminate his political opponents from

Miltiades was one of the foremost Athenian politicians and leaders and also the architect of the remarkable victory at Marathon. (Roman copy, National Museum of Ravenna)

Themistocles

69

LYKIAN MARINE IN PERSIAN ARMY SERVICE (489-479 BC)
The warriors of Asia Minor wore armor influenced by the Greeks. However, certain items such as the elaborate shield, the convex sword of type drepanon *(reaping hook), and the forked spear remain local peculiarities. (Uniform research and reconstruction - illustration by Christos Giannopoulos)*

the Athenian political scene and thus Alcmaeonid Megacles (486 BC), Xanthippos (484 BC), and finally Aristeides (482 BC) went into exile.

Victory's guide

From that moment, as the ruler of Athens, albeit in a political sense, Themistocles sought to implement his plans for the naval armament of the city, preparing it to repulse a potential Persian attack. He took advantage of a new confrontation with Athens' traditional Greek rival Aegina to propose that the annual income from the mines of Laurion – 100 talents – be used to build 100 triremes. The implementation of this proposal meant that on the eve of the Persian onslaught, Athens had a powerful battle-ready fleet of 200 triremes.

In the meantime, the Persians had begun to implement their plan, sending emissaries to Greece to demand "earth and water" (480 BC).

The time for Themistocles' glory had come. Relying on his wit and solid determination, the Athenian politician effectively "dragged" the Greeks to Salamis in order to snare the Persian fleet in an ingenious strategy that neutralized the Persians' numerical advantage and experience at war, and turned himself into the protagonist of a legendary Greek naval victory. Because of the central role Themistocles played, Herodotus, Thucydides, Plutarch, and other ancient historians give most of the credit for the victory over the "barbarians" to this Athenian commander.

His treatment by Sparta and Athens

Immediately following the Greek victory, a vote was taken to elect the bravest general and those participating in the ballot voted for Themistocles – after voting for

Themistocles' fortification works at Piraeus that were continued by Pericles. This is a representation of the Piraeus boat sheds.

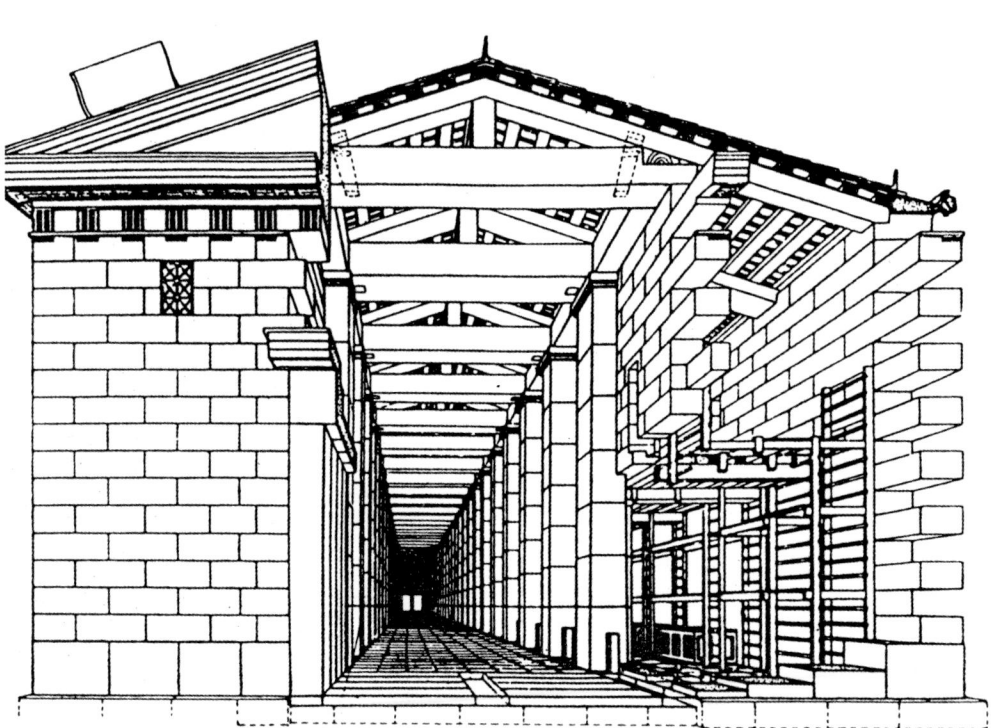

themselves first. It was the Spartans, however, who gave him the heartiest reception and showed their appreciation. When Themistocles arrived in Sparta, they crowned him with olive branches and gave him the city's finest chariot as a gift. Moreover, they also established an honor guard of 300 selected warriors to accompany him during his departure up to the borders of Tegea. At the following Olympic Games – held, probably, in 472 BC – Themistocles' arrival at the stadium distracted the spectators' attention from the athletes. Themistocles became the center of attention, receiving admiration and constant applause from the spectators, who introduced him to the foreigners attending the event – all to his great delight.

Back in Athens, however, the citizens did not demonstrate the same appreciation towards him, and this attitude probably resulted from his bad reputation and difficult character. They considered him to be avaricious and immoral, an ambitious man who missed no opportunity to show off, and who loved to be feted. According to Plutarch, after being elected admiral, he avoided dealing with any issues, public or private; postponing them all for the day when he was to set sail. Only then would he hold discussions with many people and take part in a host of last-minute activities in order to give the impression of an omnipotent, intelligent, and influential man. Whatever the case, the lack of love and gratitude shown to him by the Athenians was a matter that caused him pain and prompted him to lament bitterly that they only remembered and felt grateful for him when they were in danger. They resembled, he said, a wayfarer who took shelter from the blazing sun in the shade of a plane tree, but who was then willing to cut off the tree's branches after the sun had cooled.

As other examples of his behavior and character, Plutarch reports that when Themistocles went to sell a ranch, he ordered the town crier to spread the word that, apart from other attributes, the ranch was located next to that of an influential neighbor. Also, when it became time to marry his daughter, he preferred a man who was prudent and not rich to be the groom, saying that he preferred somebody who needed money and not money that needed somebody.

Themistocles' policy after the battle

From 479 BC, Themistocles followed an anti-Spartan policy, with the aim of strengthening the status

As a reward for his invaluable services, the Athenian people exiled Themistocles for life from his homeland. Aristeides had already been exiled a few years earlier, whereas Miltiades' son, Kimon, would share the same fate a little later. Their names were written on ceramic plates like these for ostracism.

Immediately after the Athenian victory over the Persians, Themistocles eagerly embarked on the reconstruction of Athens, rebuilding its walls using material from destroyed temples so that the Athenians would remember the disaster. This is a part of the Acropolis' northern wall.

and power of Athens. At the *amphictyonic* councils for the constitution of the First Athenian Alliance, the Spartans proposed the exclusion of those cities that had not participated in the battle against the Persians. If this were to happen, there was a danger that Thessaly, Argos, and Thebes would be excluded and Themistocles was afraid that Sparta would thereby acquire an absolute majority in the council. For this reason, he vociferously supported them, managing to convince those present that only 31 cities, most of them smaller states, had participated in the war, and that therefore, it would be a great disaster to exclude from the alliance cities from the rest of Greece. That would mean, he pointed out, that decisive power would be monopolized by just two or three major states.

The reconstruction of the city of Athens began two years after the victory in Salamis and, under Themistocles' initiative, the walls around the city began to be rebuilt. At the same time, Piraeus was fortified, a fact that constituted the crowning of the naval policy that he had supported since 493 BC. The fortification was quite advanced, when Aegina and Corinth expressed their concern to Sparta, claiming that such an action would set at risk Sparta's leading position in Greece. The Spartans agreed and immediately sent

Themistocles

The number of Athenian triremes just prior to the Battle of Salamis was approximately 200, making Athens a major naval power during the 5th Century BC. (Maritime Museum of Crete, Chania)

ambassadors to Athens with instructions to declare that the construction of walls around their city was not in the best interests of the rest of Greece, since in the event of a renewed Persian invasion, the enemy would use the fortified city of Athens, along with a number of other cities that had followed Athens' example north of Isthmus, as bases in their operations against the Peloponnese. After presenting their reasoning, the Spartans requested the immediate demolition of all the fortifications.

But Themistocles instructed the Athenians to continue their work while he sent a delegation to Sparta to discuss the issue and delay an agreement until the construction of the fortifications could be completed. The Athenians decided to send Themistocles, Aristeides, and Ambronychus to Sparta. Themistocles himself would arrive first, with the other two showing up some time later – after the fortifications were advanced enough to be able to withstand a potential Spartan invasion. As soon as Themistocles left for Sparta, the Athenian people set about with even more vigor to construct the walls, while the cunning Athenian politician delayed his meeting with the Spartan *ephors*, on the pretext that he was waiting for his two partners.

Having confidence in their former ally, the Spartans believed him, even though they continued to receive intelligence reports that the Athenian wall was growing higher by the day. Confronted with the reports, Themistocles again attempted to dissuade them by telling them not to believe the words of upstarts (who, however, were reporting actual facts), but to dispatch a delegation that could see for itself that the opposite was true. With this proposal, he wished to gain even more time and give the Athenians the opportunity to take the emissaries hostage in the event of something going wrong. In fact, the Spartans did follow his advice and, on arrival in Athens, discovered that the fortification work was almost complete, although somewhat crude due to the hastiness and inexperience of those participating in the construction. At that point,

Themistocles presented himself to the Lacedaemonians and admitted that, indeed, the City of Athens now had strong walls, both for the safety of its own citizens as well as for the safety of its allies. The Spartans now faced a fait accompli and had no choice but to accept the fortification not, of course, without expressing their dissatisfaction and bitterness. This fortification contributed in no small way to the strengthening of Athenian power both on a commercial as well as a naval level and, in combination with Pericles' policies, made Athens the protagonist of the 5th century BC.

Although Themistocles and Aristeides had divergent views for many years, they set aside their ideological differences before the common Persian threat. This is a bust of Aristeides, who was later called "the Just." (Capitolium Museum, Rome)

The ostracism

The wayward and bribery-prone character of Themistocles was never popular with the Athenians. Moreover, the Athenian people's envy for the achievements of the great victor of Salamis had not diminished and Themistocles' own attitude also contributed to this; eagerly seeking praise and honor, he missed no opportunity to remind the Athenians how much he had benefited them. Finally, in 471 or 470 BC, the Athenians decided to *ostracize* him. It was an action taken primarily to humiliate and lessen his prestige, as they believed that he had acquired too much power, something out of keeping with the democratic equality that he constantly invoked.

Themistocles took the road into exile and remained for some time in Argos, where he heard the news of the Spartans' accusation against his friend Pausanias. The latter sent a number of letters to Themistocles requesting him to cooperate and take sides with the Persian king because the Greeks were cunning and ungrateful. Themistocles turned down his proposals, but did not rush to denounce them publicly. When Pausanias was sentenced to death for high treason, documents involving Themistocles were found among his personal possessions. The Spartans at last had an opportunity to punish Themistocles for the construction of the walls against their wishes and accused him of being Pausanias' accomplice in treason because he knew about Pausanias' plans, but failed to reveal them to the people in time.

The accusations were serious and the penalty if found guilty would be death. Themistocles attempted to refute the charges, claiming that, even if he always wished to rule rather than

Themistocles

to be ruled, he would never sell his soul to the Persians or any other enemy of his homeland in general. Unfortunately, he was unable to convince his fellow-citizens. They dispatched a special delegation with orders to arrest him and bring him before them to defend himself and to be judged for the accusations with which he had been charged. Themistocles, however, being aware of their animosity, sought refuge illegally on Corfu to escape arrest.

On Artaxerxes' side

Themistocles' stay in Corfu, which he had helped in the past by reconciling it with Corinth, was brief. According to Thucydides (Book I, Ch. 1, 136) the Corfiots never accepted him, as they were afraid of the anger of his persecutors. From Corfu, Themistocles went to Epirus, where he turned to Admetus, the king of the Molossians, as a supplicant. The latter agreed to give him shelter and not hand him over to his persecutors, despite the fact that in the past the once powerful Themistocles had treated him with contempt. Then Themistocles, after passing through Pydna in Macedon, found his way to Ephesus and then Cyme in Asia Minor (today, Namurt on the west coast of Turkey). There he realized that his moves were under constant scrutiny, as the Persian king had placed 200 talents on his head. He therefore sought refuge with the eminent and affluent Nicogenes in Aegae, a small Aeolian city to the south of Cyme. Nicogenes, a wealthy man and collaborator with the Persian

Themistocles' military genius was one of the most decisive factors in the monumental Greek victory at Salamis. This is a representation of the naval Battle.

royal court, pretended that he was dispatching a beautiful Greek woman as a gift to a courtier and smuggled Themistocles out to Susa, seat of the Persian monarch, by coach. Themistocles was totally incognito and thus, everyone believed that the passenger was in fact a beautiful lady who had to be protected from the strangers' eyes according to Persian custom.

Finally, Themistocles managed to arrive at the palace of Artaxerxes. The Persian king, after overcoming his initial surprise, blessed the gods that had driven the Greeks crazy, as they wanted to eliminate their most talented general. Themistocles promised to help him subjugate Greece and, after receiving abundant examples of the Persian king's largesse, requested one year's notice

Xerxes himself was an eyewitness to the destruction of the Persian fleet at Salamis and, following the disastrous naval battle, he departed Greece. This is a relief from Persepolis Palace depicting a Persian king and his entourage.

so that he could learn the Persian language and become familiar with Persian customs. Artaxerxes showed how much he appreciated his father's former hated enemy by giving him the sum of 200 talents he had placed on his head. He then granted him the *satrapy* of Magnesia, near the Maeander River (today in western Turkey), and a number of other Persian cities from which Themistocles secured a living and where he enjoyed the pleasures of Persian life.

The end

In 465 BC, Kimon, Miltiades' son, who was the commander-in-chief of a new campaign, marked an important victory against Persian troops near the mouth of the Eurymedon River (on what is now the southern Turkish coast). After this, a rebel leader in Egypt defeated a Persian army with the help of Kimon's Athenian forces, and Artaxerxes asked Themistocles to keep his promises, assume command of the Persian forces, and move against the Athenians. Themistocles could not bear the thought of turning against his fellow-citizens; despite the bitterness he felt for the way they had treated him some years previously. Thus, according to Plutarch, after offering sacrifices to the gods and saying goodbye to his friends, he drank *taurine* (a substance found in ox bile) or some other poisonous substance that led to his death at the age of around 65. Thucydides, however, attributes his death to illness. It is a fact that not all ancient historiographers dealt with Themistocles' controversial personality in the same way. Herodotus revealed that he despised him, probably for political reasons, while, in contrast, Thucydides considered him a man of genius and worthy of admiration.

When the Persian king heard the news of the death of the great Athenian politician, he used flattering words about his character and demanded that his friends and relatives be also honored. According to Themistocles' wish, his bones were secretly transported to the Attic land and buried near the entrance of Piraeus harbor. In 1898, the archaeologist Iakovos Dragatsis claimed that Themistocles' grave was actually located on the opposite coast of Kavos Krakari.

Pausanias, the leader of the Greek forces at Plataea, was convicted of high treason and, after his death, it was revealed that he had told Themistocles of his treacherous plans, prompting the latter to flee his native land to avoid arrest. (Roman copy, Capitolium Museum, Rome)

The Persian point of view regarding the Battle of Salamis

The picture we have of the Persian Wars, and more specifically the Battle of Salamis, is inevitably limited to the Greek point of view, since there are no direct records from the Persian side. Similarly, the evaluation of the consequences of the battle reveals a Greek-centric or even a Euro-centric approach. But how important to the Achaemenian kings themselves was the defeat of the Persian fleet at Salamis? To what degree did the outcome of Xerxes' expedition influence the stability of the great king's power? Why didn't he seek to conquer Greece again? A critical approach allows a number of realistic assumptions.

The Great King listening to his subjects. This is a relief from the throne chamber of the Persepolis Palace.

During the 8th and 7th Century BC, the Assyrian kings repeatedly invaded the region of the Zagros Mountains in Eastern Mesopotamia, but the subjugation of the various local sovereigns, cities, and tribes of the region was not easy and advanced very slowly. In the late 7th Century, at the time of the Assyrian Empire's decline, a number of local sovereigns managed to unite a major part of northwestern Iran under their power, thus establishing the kingdom of Medea, with Ekbatana (modern Hamadan) as its capital. After that, they turned against Assyria along with the Babylonians and occupied Nineveh in 612 BC and Harran in 610 BC. The advance of the Medean kings continued until they reached central Anatolia. Their southerly advance was not as successful, however. During King Astyages' expedition against Cyrus, the sovereign of the kingdom of Anshan, his army revolted, defected to the enemy and deposed him. Thus Cyrus, already sovereign of the city of Anshan and leader of the local tribes, became king of Medea.

The fact that Cyrus managed to enlist Astyages' army and be accepted as king of Medea reveals much about his political competence. In 546 BC, he turned against the king of Lydia, Croesus. After an indecisive battle at the Halys River he laid siege to Croesus' capital, Sardis (modern Sart, in western Turkey), and captured his adversary. A few years later (in 539 BC) he invaded Mesopotamia, conquered Babylonia and captured its king, Nabonidus. He spent the final years of his reign subjugating the Iranian tribes of the eastern highlands. Cyrus was very indulgent with those he conquered. He granted land to the defeated rival sovereigns, restored local temples and other places of worship, assumed the local royal titles and, generally speaking, tried to appear more as an heir to the older, defeated sovereigns than their conqueror. His son and successor, Cambyses, followed the same policy: he invaded Egypt, overcame the Egyptian troops and occupied Heliopolis and Memphis. Following in his father's footsteps, Cambyses was awarded the title of Pharaoh, restored many local places of worship and temples and granted, or restored ranks to the locals, trying to gain the loyalty of his Egyptian subjects.

The extremely rapid expansion of the empire created problems of inner stability, however. There was great political rivalry, not only among the aristocrats but also within the royal family, with ranks, privileges, and prestige as a reward that finally led to open conflict and dispute with the king. The empire sank into chaos, with usurpers, regicides, and pretenders to the throne quarreling for power. In the meantime, many recently conquered regions took the opportunity to revolt, rallying around local sovereigns. Finally, a Persian aristocrat, Darius, with the support of some other Persian nobles, managed to overcome all his opponents and restore the unity of the empire under his control. Soon the new king set about legalizing his position by connecting his genealogy with that of Cyrus, founder of the empire, by means of a common ancestor, Achaemenes, and by appropriating the royal titles of the subject countries. He also had to confirm his ability as a warlord. He turned, therefore, first to

A 4th Century BC Phoenician coin bearing a relief of a warship.

the north to campaign against the Scythian tribes of central Asia, and then to the east, occupying the western bank of the Indus River. With the object of subjugating the Scythian tribes that were raiding along the borders of the empire he invaded Thrace and crossed the Danube, finally reaching the plains of modern Ukraine.

By now, the empire covered a vast area. In order to administer these immense territories, the Achaemenian kings divided it into provinces, called *satrapies*, that initially coincided with the borders of the conquered kingdoms. The administration of these provinces was assigned to trustworthy Persians, Medeans, and other aristocrats – the *satraps*. Satraps were given such extensive responsibilities and privileges that they were almost viceroys rather than simple provincial governors. Inside the *satrapies*, the governance was based upon the local elite, whose members were granted riches and ranks from the local *satrap* or the King. The provincial administration's basic mission was to preserve the peace and to collect the taxes and forward them to the capital. The King, meanwhile, governed his empire and supervised the *satraps* from his two capitals, Susa and Persepolis, surrounded by trustworthy "relatives" and "attendants."

The Great King on his throne, supported by his attendants. Above him flies Ahura Mazda. This is a relief from the central chamber of the Persepolis Palace.

The Achaemenian kings relied mainly on their army to impose their will. During the first years of Cyrus and Darius, the army appeared to have a somewhat feudal structure. The support of the Persian aristocracy, and by extension, the Persian tribes, was necessary to enable the king to be in a position to mobilize his military forces. Later, the need to free the central government from the tribal warlords and the wish to form a reliable military mechanism, led to the organization of a regular army, called the Immortals, which consisted of 10,000 Persians, Medeans, and Elamites under the direct command of the Great King. At the same time, *cleruchies* and local guards made up of mercenaries were maintained across the whole empire, especially in Egypt and Mesopotamia. In the provinces, the *satraps* were allowed to establish their own armed escorts and recruit their local subjects whenever required. A complicated mechanism of logistics took care of the army's catering during an expedition – near the coasts, transport ships with naval protection saw to the supply of the army.

The Persian point of view regarding the Battle of Salamis

Xerxes' tomb at Persepolis.

Whatever the situation, the king appeared as the supreme warlord. In his titles and monumental iconography, the King prevailed as a horseman, archer, hunter, conqueror of cities and peoples. He was the chosen one of the Great God, Ahura Mazda, and undertook the mission to restore the divine unity and order of the world. His infrastructure worked not only as a military machine, however, but also as a means of peaceful coexistence – he constructed temples and palaces, canals and irrigation ditches throughout the empire, ensuring not only the prosperity of his subjects but also enhancing his own prestige. He was the fair sovereign, the protector of his subjects, the Pharaoh of Egypt, the king of Babylonia and local sovereign of all the other countries he had conquered. His generosity could forgive almost anything apart from treason. Mutineers received exemplarily punishments: slaughter, destruction of their temples, and slavery were the usual means of punishment for those who disputed the order of the King and of the Supreme God that protected him. The emphasis on the punishment of the mutineers was especially extreme during the reign of Xerxes, son and heir of Darius, who faced many revolts during his first years on the throne.

Of course, the gulf between royal propaganda and political reality can be enormous. It is important to understand the ideology of the Achaemenians and the mechanism of legitimizing their power that was based on a mixture of benefits and intimidation. Especially, in the case of either revolt or military defeat, the need to re-establish royal prestige before the eyes of his subjects was imperative in order to prevent the emergence of any rebellious attitudes in the future. In consequence, a direct counter-attack and exemplary punishment of the enemies were the only options for the Great King.

The Achaemenians and the Greek cities

The Greek cities of western Asia Minor had been subjugated to the Achaemenians since the middle of the 6th Century BC, when the Persian army reached the region in order to break up the Lydian kingdom. In the late 6th Century, when Darius occupied Thrace, the Greek coastal cities of the region of the Northern Aegean, Hellespont, and the Black Sea were also subjugated. The Achaemenians encouraged the appointment of sovereigns (*tyrants*) in these cities, in order to supervise and control them more effectively. The revolt of the Ionian and Cypriot cities during the period from 499 to 494 BC was one of many uprisings that occasionally broke out within the empire. Although the rebels managed to raze Sardis, the provincial capital, the revolt was quickly suppressed. In order to re-establish royal power over the Greek cities of the European satrapy, Skudra (which included the European territories of the empire), Mardonius, the king's trusted general, campaigned in Thrace and Macedonia in 492 BC.

The Ionian cities had not revolted on their own, being supported by small forces from Athens and Eretria, two Greek cities on the opposite mainland. Punishing these foreigners, who were interfering in the Great King's affairs, was for the king a matter of prestige: a fleet sailed from Ionia, occupied Naxos, subjugated the rest of the Cyclades and Karystos on Euboea and landed its army at Eretria. The city was besieged and, after betrayal, was finally occupied, its residents sent into slavery and exile in Mesopotamia. The Persian expeditionary force then landed at the Marathon Plain in Athenian territory, where it suffered defeat in the ensuing battle because its cavalry was unable to exploit its superiority. Despite the loss, the Great King did not regard the expedition a failure. Apart from the "minor" setback at Marathon, he had placed the central Aegean Sea under his control and had made a powerful example of one the cities that had challenged his sovereignty. Although Herodotus reports that he intended to return, the Aegean front was of absolutely secondary importance at that time.

As previously mentioned, Xerxes, who succeeded Darius, faced many revolts. A few months before the death of Darius, a revolt had already broken out in Egypt (486 BC). The new king headed for the region with his army and quickly suppressed the uprising. In the meantime, news of another revolt, this time by the Babylonians, arrived and General Megabyzus was sent to Mesopotamia where he successfully extinguished this rising as well, in 484 or 482 BC. These revolts convinced Xerxes that he had to rule his empire with an iron fist and, certainly, with less tolerance for those who defied him than his predecessors had exhibited. His brother, Achaemenes, was appointed satrap of Egypt, the property of many temples was confiscated, while Xerxes abandoned the title of Pharaoh and the obligations that emanated from it towards the Egyptians. Babylonia's fate was even harsher. Its walls and a number of temples were demolished, its priests were executed, and the

The Persian point of view regarding the Battle of Salamis

Ionian subjects of the Great King bring him gifts. This is a relief from the throne chamber of the Persepolis Palace.

statue of the patron god Marduk was removed. It is no accident that, during his reign, the official propaganda inscriptions stressed the importance of the traitors' punishment and the imposition of the divine order of Ahura Mazda. In this way, political loyalty was connected to religion, being identified with acknowledging the primacy of the supreme Persian god.

After re-establishing his power within the empire, Xerxes obviously realized that military success outside the empire's borders during the first years of his reign was imperative in order to confirm the traditional role of the conqueror king. An expedition against Greece was considered a good solution. Greece was split into small cities and there were no really powerful states. Various Greek exiles had reached the Persian Court and asked for the Great King's support in order to return as sovereigns to their homelands. The punishment of Athens, the second city that had helped the Ionians during their revolt, also served as a good pretext. In any case, Xerxes could not have fixed his gaze on the economic importance of these cities or, indeed, on their potential as a source of tax revenue, because, by the standards of the empire, they were negligible. In addition, their military or naval forces were certainly not powerful enough to constitute any substantial threat to the Great King. So, in consequence, it was only their preventive elimination that was important. The Greek cities actually appeared to be easy prey for the Great King.

In 480 BC, the king assembled his troops at Sardis, the capital of the nearest Asiatic *satrapy*, and afterwards at Doriscus in Thrace. Herodotus certainly exaggerated when he wrote about "millions" of men; but whatever the real number of troops, the Great King's force was the largest army that had invaded the Greek region until then. It surely included the 10,000 Immortals, several elite units of cavalry and guards, as well as Medeans, Bactrians, Sakas, Indians, and others; all of them were professional soldiers, infantry and cavalry. Also, the king's subjects from those countries closest to the area of conflict (Mysia, Phrygia, Thrace, Paeonia, and Macedonia) were recruited. At the same time, a huge fleet was assembled on the Ionian coasts, consisting of many triremes and other ships from Egypt, Phoenicia, Cyprus, and Ionia. Their crews were reinforced with Persian, Medean, and Saka soldiers. The support and catering of this huge force constituted a great logistical accomplishment, while the support works that allowed its advance through Greece were also equally important. Two bridges united the Dardanelle coasts to facilitate the crossing of the army, while a canal was later constructed across the foot of the Athos peninsula to allow the fleet to pass through safely.

The reaction of the Greek cities was spasmodic: they hastily ordered a division of the allied army at Tempe to stop the Persians from venturing deep into the Greek region. When Xerxes by-passed the narrow area, however, the allied army withdrew. The cities of Thessaly were subjugated and reinforced the Great King's army. A smaller Greek allied force had reached Thermopylae under the command of the king of Sparta, Leonidas. It was a matter of prestige for Xerxes to occupy this narrow area, but the first assaults by his elite units were repulsed. Finally, a mountain path allowed him to by-pass this narrow area also, and to eliminate the few Spartans and Thespians who had opted to make a stand rather than withdraw south with the others. The occupation of Thermopylae also forced the Greek allied fleet, whose mission it was to prevent the descent of the Persian fleet into Artemisium, to withdraw to the south.

The Great King also subjugated the cities of Boeotia. The same happened to the Phocians and, probably, to the Temple of Delphi, despite the stories of miraculous intervention by the god Apollo that the priests later spread with the purpose of protecting the prestige of the Pan-Hellenic sanctuary. The Persian army invaded Attica unhindered. Facing the danger of annihilation, the Athenians, abandoning their city, transported the old men, women, and children to the islands and to the opposite coasts of the Argosaronic Bay and then took to their ships that had been arrayed, along with the rest of the allied fleet, at the nearby island of Salamis. Athens was leveled and its temples razed. Ahura Mazda once again triumphed over the "false" gods. Xerxes sent news of Athens' fall to Susa, where it was enthusiastically received.

The Peloponnesian allies wished at that point to make a stand at Isthmus with their army and fleet, while the Athenian general Themistocles set about convincing them rather to fight a naval battle in the narrow passage of Salamis. For his part, Xerxes wanted an immediate, decisive, and glorious victory, as autumn was approaching. Those among the Great King's entourage most experienced in naval issues agreed. The preparations for the attack had probably already begun when a Greek fugitive, sent by

The Persian point of view regarding the Battle of Salamis

Themistocles, reported to Xerxes that the Greeks were arguing anew and that it was the perfect opportunity to crush them. That night, the Egyptian fleet was sent to cut off the western exit towards Megara, while the Phoenician and Ionian fleets were sent to the east, to the side of Attica. An elite force landed on the nearby islet of Psyttaleia in order to kill any Greek castaways and rescue the Persian ones.

At dawn, under the eye of the Great King and his escort, who had set up their observation post on Mount Aegaleo, the Persian fleet entered the strait with the rising sun at its back. The Greeks, who had been informed of the blockade during the night, hurried to man their ships and set sail. Faced with the attacking Persian fleet, the Greek triremes began a tactical withdrawal, thus deceiving the king's ships and drawing them deeper inside the narrow strait. When the Greek counter-attack began, the Phoenician and Ionian ships, jammed in a narrow area, were unable to put their naval experience into effect. Confusion followed, as the ships of the secondary ranks continued their attack only to collide with the vessels from their own front ranks when the latter began a tactical relocation. By the afternoon, the Persian fleet had suffered a humiliating defeat, losing, according to Diodorus Siculus, 200 ships as well as the elite guard on Psyttaleia. Ariabignes, commander-in-chief of the fleet and the King's brother, was among the Persians killed in action that day.

After Salamis

Xerxes, however, did not give up. Despite his battle losses and storms, his fleet was still a formidable force. The Greek allies were aware of this and waited, safe inside the strait, for a second attack that was expected soon after the first. But the king assembled his ships at Phaleron and ordered that a jetty, already under construction before the battle, be extended with the aim of connecting Perama with Salamis, so that his army could mount an assault and occupy the island. At the same time, his cavalry advanced from Eleusis to Megaris and Isthmus ravaging the countryside as it went. Apparently, during this time, Poseidon's temple at Isthmia was also razed. In the meantime, hunkered behind the wall that they had built, the Peloponnesians waited for the Great King's attack. The attack, however, never materialized.

The jetty connecting Perama to Salamis was not completed. The harsh autumn winds prevented the fleet from remaining at sea, preventing any

The Great King followed by his attendants. This is a relief from the palace of Xerxes at Persepolis.

of the planned operations from taking place, and, with winter fast approaching, Xerxes decided to return to Sardis to set up his winter camp there and prepare for a new round of battle the following year. An elite force remained in Greece under Mardonius, the Great King's trustworthy general, while he left the royal tent and Ahura Mazda's chariot in Europe, as proof that he intended to return. On the other hand, the Persian fleet returned to Ionia and the Eastern Mediterranean, although the Greek allies were unable to take advantage of its absence and retake control of the Cyclades. It appears that Xerxes considered that the army already located in Greece and the reinforcements that would probably arrive the following spring sufficient to subjugate the Peloponnese without the help of the fleet.

Despite all these preparations, the Achaemenian king did not return to Greece the following year. After the Persian defeat at Salamis, anti-Persian sentiments in the Ionian cities were rekindled. Perhaps Xerxes preferred to remain at Sardis as a show of strength to intimidate possible mutineers and immediately confront any revolt – although it appears that rumblings of discontent did not only exist in Ionia. Meanwhile, Mardonius sought to force the Greeks to engage in a battle at Boeotia, where his cavalry would be able to perform or, better still, assure the subjugation of the Athenians. Finally, the Lacedaemonians and their allies, fearful that the Athenians might defect to the Persians, agreed to advance to the north of Isthmus, up to Plataea on the outskirts of Boeotia. The Greeks remained in their positions for many days, apprehensive of an open battle against the Persian cavalry on the plain. Mardonius, who wished for a decisive victory before diminishing supplies forced him to withdraw, finally attacked with all his forces in August of 479 BC. The result of the fierce battle that followed was that his army was defeated and he himself killed. The remnants of the Persian army then finally withdrew from Greek soil. Almost simultaneously, the allied fleet arrived at Ionia, where the region's Persian fleet lay at anchor. The *epibatae* (marines) of both fleets fought on land, at Cape Mycale, and once again the Persians were defeated and their fleet burnt. Seeing this, the Ionian cities were further encouraged and revolted; a little later Xerxes hastily withdrew from Sardis.

What was, however, the real reason for his withdrawal? It seems that the Great King wanted to control the situation up to the last moment, either by preparing a new expedition against Greece or by closely supervising the Ionian cities. Why, then, did he withdraw without attempting a counter-attack? It is very likely that at that moment, another revolt broke out in Babylonia, perhaps fueled by the military failures of the king in the West. Our sources with regard to Babylonia's facts are vague, but it can be reasonably assumed that the revolt was in support of a man called Shamash-eriba, who proclaimed himself king of Babylonia at that time. Something of this nature would surely justify Xerxes' hasty departure to Mesopotamia, as re-establishing his power inside the empire was far more important than the conquest of the Greek cities. Whatever the reason, the fact remains that Xerxes never returned to Greece.

The planned new *satrapy* of Greece was lost for the Great King at Plataea and not at Salamis, as the Persian military presence remained substantially intact and a threat to

Greece until August 479 BC. The undeniable pro-Athenian attitude of Herodotus explains the particular importance he attributes to the Battle of Salamis, and it is this that influenced historians in later times. Similarly, the almost simultaneous Persian defeat at Mycale in Asia Minor, even if it was of a relatively small scale, resulted in the secession of the Ionian cities. In the following years, Xerxes not only did not attempt a new expedition in the Aegean and in Greece, but also rather watched as his territories in Asia Minor were attacked by the Spartans and later by the Athenians and their allies. Actually, in 467 BC, the allied Greek fleet under Kimon from Athens struck a decisive blow against the Persian fleet at the Eurymedon River in Pamphylia, now on the southern coast of Turkey.

Two years later, Xerxes the Great King, was murdered by members of his own court. Until then, however, neither the defeats in Greece, the revolts of the Ionian cities, nor the Athenian attacks that followed across the entire Eastern Mediterranean, had managed to undermine the Achaemenian king. In fact, there were no further reports of revolts or usurpers contesting his power from anywhere across his still vast empire. On the contrary, during the final 15 years of his life, Xerxes focused his energies on the completion of his brilliant palace at Persepolis. Everything known about the Persian Empire at this time confirms the fact that the Persian king had stopped being truly interested in the West and Greece in particular following the disastrous defeats of his army and fleet.

Official inscriptions concerning Xerxes reveal that he still considered himself ruler of Thrace ("Skudra") and of "the Ionians here and beyond the sea," that is, the Greeks on both sides of the Aegean. Besides, the Great King had victoriously advanced up to Isthmus, had subjugated all the Greek cities in his path (albeit temporarily), had won a battle and taken the life of the Spartan king and, finally, he had conquered and destroyed Athens in reprisal for its role during the Ionian Revolt and for the Persian defeat at Marathon. Even the destruction of the Athenian temples appears as an act of vengeance for the fall of Sardis and the razing of its temples by the Ionians and the Athenians in 498 BC. Looking at it in this way, Xerxes could reasonably consider his Greek expedition to be a "success."

The King's claims on Thrace and, furthermore, on Greece lack any substantial basis, but they were consistent with the widespread self-promotion of the Achaemenians as invincible warlords and world rulers. Besides, even the temporary subjugation of a region was a more vivid demonstration of royal power before the eyes of the king's subjects than would be any meager material income (won at disproportionately great cost) that might result from a permanent conquest. The Persian claims upon Ionia had a quite different character. The truth is that the Persian kings never relinquished their dominion over the Ionian cities of the Eastern Aegean, until they were finally recovered by Artaxerxes II in the "King's Peace" of 386 BC. The interventionist role of the Achaemenians in the conflicts among the Greek cities was made official in the same treaty, thus sealing a process that had already begun during the years of the Peloponnesian War and was to last up to Alexander the Great's campaign in the East. In the end, the Persian King's gold accomplished what his archers and triremes could not.

"Themistocles' Trophy" and the "Salamis Warriors' tomb"

In search of the heroes' bones

According to Diodorus, during the Battle of Salamis the Greeks lost roughly 40 ships. This means that at least 8,000 men, oarsmen, seamen, and *epibatae* (marines) fell or leapt into the sea. The majority of them could swim and thus managed to reach the shore on the nearby, safe island of Salamis. Many, however, must have been killed during the clashes on the ships or drowned when they were caught in the maelstroms of the sinking ships. Those who did not go down with their ships were buried by their comrades-in-arms in Salamis. The Persians did not, however, meet the same fate, as they either could not swim or were killed by the Greeks, who struck them unmercifully with their oars and pushed them below the surface.

Herodotus does not reveal the position of the site where the fallen Greek soldiers and sailors from the battle were buried. The records that do exist are from quite some time later and, in consequence, their reliability is questionable. It is known that a few years after the naval battle, Athenian youngsters danced around the trophy accompanied by the playing of lyres. Among them there was fifteen-year-old Sophocles, the future great tragic poet. Later, the Athenian teenagers participated in a ritual mission each year: they rowed up to the ancient city of Salamis in order to perform a sacrifice to Ajax and, during their return, they stopped at the trophy of

A current view of the Salamis warriors' tomb.

"Themistocles' Trophy" and the "Salamis Warriors' tomb"

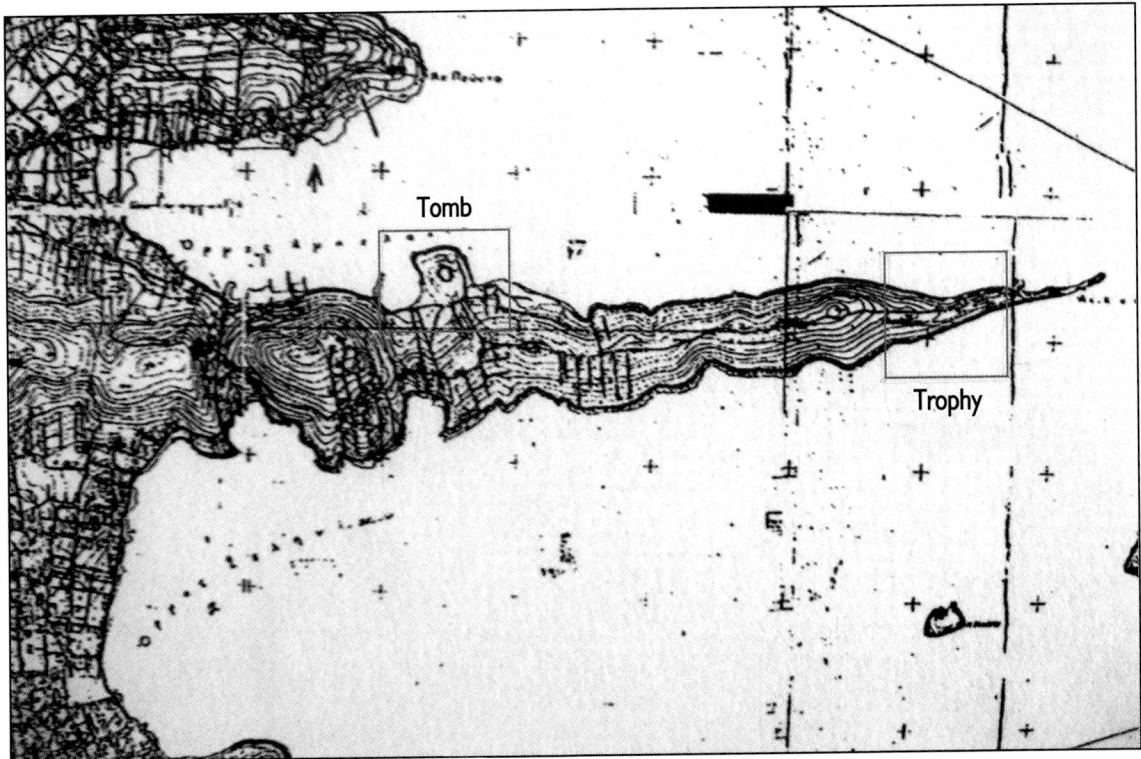

A topographical chart of Ampelakia and Kynosoura Bay, showing the sites of the tomb and the trophy.

the naval battle, where they sacrificed to Zeus. A fragmentary inscription of the time of Octavian Augustus refers to "Themistocles' trophy" and the nearby *polyandreion*. The latter obviously refers to the common grave of the fallen Athenian *epibatae* and seamen of the battle who were probably all buried together. Under such conditions and with so many men dead, their recognition and burial according to their cities would have been extremely difficult; therefore there must have been a common Pan-Hellenic grave. Nevertheless, we know that the Corinthians were authorized to bury their own fallen *epibatae* and seamen near the city of Salamis, probably in a separate grave, while they built a *cenotaph* in their homeland dedicated to all their fellow citizens who were killed in the battles during 480 and 479 BC. This is a good example of evidence revealing that to the ancient Greeks, the individual was of secondary importance to that of his or her city.

Neither the position of Themistocles' trophy and the relevant common grave, nor the precise topography of the region where the battle took place has been completely clarified. Even though N. G. L. Hammond preferred to identify the cape where the trophy had been located with the peninsula of Kamatero, at the north of Ampelakia, foreign travelers had already described the remains of a marble monument at Cape Kynosoura, south of Ampelakia, which were still visible from the opposite coast as late as the 18th Century. This second rocky peninsula was probably called Kychreia in antiquity. A flat surface was quite recently discovered on the rock at the eastern end of the peninsula at a point 10 meters above the ground. It had sculptured notches used as sockets for stone blocks, which obviously constituted the monument that was visible until the 19th Century. Unfortunately, very little of the materials used in its construction were rescued, as many of them were removed over the centuries – some actually turning up in Venice. It appears, however, from the descriptions by those travelers that there had been at least one pillar erected upon an established base.

Given the trophy's position, the common grave should also have been located at the Kynosoura peninsula. The tomb of Magoula, that roughly dominates the center of the peninsula, is one of the more likely candidates. Nevertheless, a small-scale excavation in the 1960s on and around the tomb revealed only a few graves from the late 5th Century BC, dating, in fact, from over 50 years after the historical naval battle, and located on the periphery of the hill. In any case, its form refers to a human construction, namely a tomb and not just a hillock that probably existed before those late 5th Century BC graves. The stone structures discovered next to the graves and the tomb – probably the remains of some altar – actually imply that the area had a devotional character. Does this construction constitute a sign of idolization and adoration of the fallen marines and seamen of the naval battle, relative to that of the Marathon warriors? Unfortunately, neither was the altar precisely dated, nor was the excavation extended in order to clarify the area's character, while independent historical records concerning the later adoration of the warriors of Salamis are also absent. Under these conditions, the altar was reasonably identified with the sanctuary of a local hero, Kychreas, who, according to legend, took part in the battle on the side of the Athenians.

The 1st Century inscription concerning the restorations of Attica's temples, leads us to the conclusion that the entire cape was considered to be sacred at that time; an area that was consecrated by the heroes of the mythical and historical past of Athens, that had to be protected from the usurpation of private individuals whose properties appeared to trespass dangerously on the once historic area. Besides, the time of the announcement of this resolution does not appear to be accidental: following the end of the Roman civil wars, Athens tried to recover from the recession by showing off its history and cultural heritage to the new sovereign of Rome and Greece, Octavian. Indeed, the city continued to be recognized as the new intellectual metropolis by the new ruling class and enjoyed special privileges. The proud promotion of a communal, or Pan-Hellenic identity through the use of the glorious past was a generalized phenomenon throughout Greece during the Roman era. It expressed the intention to safeguard the moral independence of the Greek cities, and especially Athens, in a new historical situation in which any political independence had been long forgotten.

What is the region's situation today? The Archaeological Department has, since 1964 – 1966, already declared the Kynosoura region an area of archaeological interest and, in 2001, certain areas of the region were more precisely determined as protected from the intervention of any construction. Various facilities had already been built on the peninsula several years earlier, however, and nowadays the region is the property of a large company. A proposal concerning the expropriation of the area, so that excavations and the improvement of the area could continue, crashed when the cost reached 1,000,000,000 *drachmas* in 1993 (around US$4.5 million). Given the Ministry of

"Themistocles' Trophy" and the "Salamis Warriors' tomb"

"The Victors of Salamis." A romantic representation of the spirit that prevailed after the great naval battle.

Culture's low budget – the lowest of any Greek Ministry – along with the pressing needs for expropriations in other areas, the delay of the expropriation of the region of the "tomb" should come as no surprise.

Much fuss is made concerning the improvement of the area, a fact that often serves political expedience as well as personal ambition. This issue frequently shows up in the local and/or the Athenian Press, even though the situation is seldom sufficiently explained. Without doubt, however, the rhetoric surrounding the importance of the battle (and, by extension, of the monument itself) is a potent reminder of the climate in Athens during Octavian's reign, when the city attempted to remind everyone of its glorious past in compensation for its miserable present. The picture of the region, as well as of many other archaeological sites in Greece today is, undisputedly, lamentable, (for example, the cement dust that is corroding the monuments at Eleusis and the rowing center at Marathon). Before placing the blame on the state for its insufficiency, however, consideration by all for respect of the historical heritage is vital. The quality of our education and ethics is also reflected in the way we treat, as private individuals and as citizens, our past and its monuments.

Whether this tomb actually covers the bones of the Athenian "Salamis warriors" or was simply a sanctuary of local hero Kychreas, still remains a mystery. The truth is that, apart from Magoula's tomb, there are no other sites on the cape that can be considered as candidates for the identification of a common grave. A more systematic excavation will put an end to the discussions and speculations and will reveal to us the actual character of the tomb.

It must be said however that the majority of the fallen heroes of the naval Battle, both Greeks and Persians, ended up at the bottom of the sea in the narrow passage of Salamis along with their ships and they are today covered by thousands of tons of mud and other products of our modern way of life.

Lesser-known details of the Battle of Salamis

In a battle of such a great importance, it is completely understandable that the incidents that preceded and those that followed Salamis were blown out of all proportion, while many various events, either actual or imagined, have been related in narrative accounts. Many of them, thanks to Plutarch, have been preserved.

- A long time before the glorious conflict at Salamis, the ambitious Themistocles, who was an Athenian politician, stressed to his friends that Miltiades' success in Marathon kept him awake at night ("Miltiades' trophy would not let me sleep," according to Plutarch).
- During the great battle between the Greeks and the Asians, the Oracle of Delphi, pondering in cold realism over the forces of the two opponents, had obviously sided with the Persians, and prompted the Greeks to make peace with the intruders. The Oracle gave various prophecies, all of them pointing in this direction. The one that was given to the determined Athenian delegation, however, left some room for the hope of victory. It explicitly mentioned the Island of Salamis in particular – a fact that provoked very profound discussions. The prophecy, of course, could be interpreted in one way or another as usual: "... some other time you will also stand face to face with them (the intruders). Oh, Divine Salamis, you will bring death to women's sons when the corn is scattered, or the harvest gathered in." Who precisely the children of women were who were to be destroyed in the sea of Salamis' was not clarified, nor was the precise time (autumn or summer). This statement, whatever it meant, was enough for a dynamic leader such as Themistocles to use as it served him, promoting his own interpretation.
- During the dramatic hours of the evacuation of Athens, Xanthippos, one of the leaders of the democratic party (and Pericles' father), boarded a ship together with his family and the few things they could carry and sailed to Salamis, leaving, of course, the house and all their other belongings at the mercy of the intruders. His faithful dog, Xuthus, however, did not wish to remain in Athens, preferring to accompany his masters. He, thus, followed them and jumped into the sea, where he swam next to the boat until it reached Salamis. Exhausted by the effort, he passed away near his sad owners. They buried the faithful animal near the anchorage and, perhaps, this is why the particular point of the island was called *Kynos sema* (dog's grave).
- During those difficult hours, Themistocles demonstrated his political acumen once again (according to a testimony again recorded by Plutarch). Because the state was in great need of money, he compelled the most affluent citizens to make a contribution. According to one version, while the citizens were leaving, a rumor was spread that the Gorgoneion from Athena's statue had disappeared. Then Themistocles ordered the examination of all baggage the Athenians had with them under the pretext of searching for the thief. In this way he discovered a lot of money, which he seized and later shared among the soldiers and sailors. According to another version recorded by Aristotle, however, the *Areios Pagos* Supreme (the Supreme Court of Appeal which was constituted by the old aristocrats) willingly gave eight obols (an ancient Greek monetary unit) to each soldier.
- The disagreement between the Greek commanders prior to the naval battle was the source for many arguments. In the most characteristic one,

Lesser-known details

Eurybiades, who was particularly irritated by Themistocles' insistence, or perhaps by certain contemptuous words as well, raised his Spartan baton in order to hit him. At this, Themistocles calmly responded: "Hit me but listen to me." In another instance, at the beginning of the second meeting called by Eurybiades, Themistocles immediately began talking and expressed his opinion. Then, Adeimantus of Corinth pointed out to him that, "At the games, the athletes that start before the sign is given, are slapped in the face," which elicited the fast retort by the witty Athenian, "Yes, but those who delay, do not win." According to Plutarch, this dialogue was exchanged between Themistocles and Eurybiades and not Adeimantus. Plutarch also mentions the incident of the threatened blow, wishing to stress the rage caused to the Spartan by the answer it elicited. Themistocles' intelligence and the significant experience he had acquired from relevant personal attacks or recriminations at the *Ecclesia* of the City of Athens are obvious in such incidents. In these military councils it appears that Themistocles did not enjoy the support he expected from the Greeks whose cities were in direct danger (Chalcis, Eretria, Megara, Aegina). This is the reason why, when the leader of the Eretrians expressed an opinion, he immediately rebuked him saying, "You speak of war, you who have a knife as the squids, but you do not have a heart."

● Plutarch, however, also records a strange story. He says that, a little while before the naval battle when Themistocles prepared himself in order to sacrifice to the gods, the soothsayer Euphrantides suggested he should sacrifice three eminent Persian captives, the children of Artauctes and Sandake (Xerxes' sister), as this would supposedly predispose the god Dionysus to favor the Greeks. The three captives had been arrested during the assault of Aristeides' men on Psyttaleia. Thus, the human sacrifice was carried out even though the Athenian leader did not at first agree; finally, the pressure of his soldiers who had been influenced by the soothsayer's prophecies convinced him. This story reached Plutarch by Phanias of Lesbos, who had discovered it in Persica by Ctesias from Cnidus. Given, however, that the Greek attack on Psyttaleia was carried out after the main battle in the strait, it was impossible for the supposed victims to have been captured there previously and, moreover, as Ctesias is an unreliable source due to his exaggerations, we must come to the conclusion that this incident is probably untrue.

● A little while before the battle, in the evening when the Persian triremes blocked the Greek fleet, the Athenian politician Aristeides, son of Lysimachos who was exiled on Aegina, noticed the Asians' move and hurriedly sailed to Salamis to report it to the leaders of the allied fleet. When the military council ended, having made the decision to fight the battle there, the two foremost political opponents, Themistocles of the democratic party and Aristeides of the aristocratic one, were left alone. The two men eagerly agreed to stand side by side for the sake of their homeland. Plutarch actually remarks that Themistocles, "Acknowledging Aristeides' honesty and being very excited because he had accepted to side with him, revealed the secret to him with the help of Siccinus and warmly prompted him to help change the Greeks' opinion and show the same eagerness with him as far as his plan was concerned, so that they would fight the battle in the passage... Aristeides agreed with him and went to the other generals and *trierarchs* and prompted them to fight the battle there..."

● The Ionians, who were lined up on the left flank of the Persian battle array with 150 to 200 ships, even if they were Greeks fighting against Greeks, did not lower their

Lesser-known details

standards as far as doing battle was concerned, as Themistocles had prompted them after Artemisium; on the contrary, they proved to be very capable opponents of their compatriots. They fought hard and caused considerable losses to the allied naval force. The case of a trireme from Samothrace is characteristic. It rammed and sank an Athenian ship but was then attacked and destroyed by an Aeginian trireme that had hurried to assist its Aeginian colleagues. The Corinthians on board their ship were experienced javelin throwers, however, and using these, they massacred the entire crew of the enemy trireme with a continuous rain of missiles as their own ship was sinking and slipped away on the captured ship. Of course, it is more likely that they killed the sailors and the epibatae and not all the oarsmen, as undertaking that would require a lot of time, which they probably did not have. The attitude of the Ionians, as well as the Boeotians and Thessalians and all the others who sided with Mardonius at Plataea to fight against their allied compatriots, sheds particular light on the importance of the participation of Greek mercenaries in the Persian army, who later confronted Alexander the Great's Pan-Hellenic expedition. Those who are astonished at this participation are obviously not fully aware of the history of the Greek – Persian Wars of the 5th Century BC.

● From the total of 382 Greek warships (368 triremes and 14 penteconters) the overwhelming majority came from the states of metropolitan Greece (379), while only one ship had come from the colonies of the West, which was the trireme of Phayllus from Sicily's Croton, and two triremes from the East (one of Lemnos and one from Tenos or Tenedos with Panaitios as captain).

● Artemisia, the queen of Halicarnassus, a vassal of Xerxes, was the protagonist in many incidents. Firstly, at the Persian councils, she always spoke with courage and did not hesitate to oppose or even disagree with the king. As a matter of fact, she was the only one who objected to the decision to enter the narrow passage. According to her opinion, they (the Persians) should let the Greeks disband of their own accord because of the dissension among them and their extreme provincialism. When she herself was later found in the battle as the leader of her small squadron, she not only demonstrated courage but also cunning. Obviously, because of her virtues, the Athenians had placed a considerable amount of money (10,000 Attic *drachmas*.) on her head in advance. At the moment of the Persian withdrawal, an Athenian ship (with Ameinias of Dekeleia as captain) located and pursued her. The cunning queen, however, suddenly dashed ahead and rammed the ship in front of her to elude her pursuer, even though it was on her own side. Indeed, it was the king of the Calyndians' ship that was caught off guard and sank with all hands. Artemisia's wretched action created contradicting impressions within the overall confusion; the Athenian captain believed he had a friendly ship in front of him, therefore he did not continue with the pursuit, while Xerxes, forlornly watching the defeat of his fleet, thought that she fought bravely. It appears that precise identification - "friend or foe" - in the chaos of the clash between almost similar ships was not easy. In any case, Artemisia gained the favor of her king, who said with a sigh, "My men became women and my women became men." But, beyond this negative incident, Xerxes had another opportunity to appreciate the shrewd queen, when she located and pulled from the sea the dead Admiral Ariamenes, the Persian king's brother.

Lesser-known details

- During the dramatic moments of the pursuit of the Asians who were trying to escape, the trireme of the Athenian leader, Themistocles, was found near a trireme of the Aeginians, commanded by the courageous and most capable Polycritus. When Polycritus recognized the ship of the Athenian admiral (from the several signs it probably carried), he took the opportunity to shout at him: "Themistocles, who said that the Aeginians side with the Persians?"

- Herodotus also recorded the testimony of an Athenian exile called Dicaeus, son of Theocydes, according to whom he and Demaratus from Sparta, another exile, observed a strange phenomenon as they visited the Thriasion field before the great battle. A large dust cloud had been raised, precisely like the one during the procession of the 30,000 Athenians that followed the *Hiera Odos* (Sacred Road) to Eleusis at the time of festival. At the same time, they heard mysterious voices, like those that the faithful heard when they made invocations to Iacchus. The two Greek exiles were alarmed and jointly agreed to report nothing to the Persian king, as they thought that these signs foretold a disaster for the Asians and a victory for the Greeks in the forthcoming confrontation. The great cloud of dust, from which the voices were heard, appeared to be moving toward the Greek camp in Salamis. "Thus they realized, it says, that the navy of Xerxes was destined to be destroyed." Plutarch also records the same story, although a little differently, as he adds that, "others believed that they clearly saw ghosts and shades of armed men that came with hands outstretched from Aegina towards the side where the Greek ships were anchored. The Aeacidae said that they were the armed men that the Greeks had called for help before the battle."

- After this momentously important battle and during the celebrations following their victory, the Greeks decided to grant awards (*aristeion*, meaning high distinction) to the cities and to the men that had distinguished themselves. Among the cities, Aegina received the first award. Ameinias of Athens and Polycritus of Aegina were elected the foremost among the captains. The culmination of the process for the choice of the greatest leader was characteristic. As each of the generals voted for... himself, no one was elected the first winner. Because they all voted for Themistocles as second, however, he was elected as the best general, even though he came second in the ballot. What the military leaders, because of their egotism, did not recognize, the simple people did with abundant enthusiasm. During the Olympic Games of that year (480 BC), that were obviously undertaken without delay, whenever Themistocles entered the stadium where the events were taking place, all the spectators "stopped being interested in the athletes and looked at him and showed him to the foreigners and applauded him, full of admiration for the rest of the day," (Plutarch). Similarly, the proud Spartans, proving that they could indeed recognize ethical principles, invited the Athenian leader to their city (an exceptionally rare occurrence) in order to present Eurybiades the prize of bravery and the prize of wisdom, a wreath made from olive branches. Moreover, they gave Themistocles the finest chariot that had been manufactured in their city (which was famous for the quality of its war chariots), and, when it was time for him to depart, 300 elite Spartan warriors (also known as the *hippeis*, meaning equestrians) accompanied him to the borders of Laconia.

Bibliography

Aeschylus. *The Persians*, play included in volume entitled: *Prometheus Bound / the Suppliants / Seven against Thebes / the Persians*. (Translated by Philip Vellacott) London, New York: Penguin, 1961.

Amouretti, Marie-Claire and Françoise Ruzé. *Koinonia kai polemos stin archaia Ellada, (Society and War in ancient Greece)*. Athens: Patakis Publications, 2001.

Amouretti, Marie-Claire and Françoise Ruzé. *Les Sociétés grecques et la guerre à l'époque classique*. Paris: Ellipses Édition Marketing, c1999.

Barell, R. *Oi Ellines*, (The Greeks). Athens: Rossis Publications, 1994.

Briant, Pierre. *Histoire de l'Empire perse: de Cyrus à Alexander*. Paris: Fayard, 1996.

Bury, John Bagnell, and Meiggs, Russell. *Istoria tis Archaias Elladas, History of Ancient Greece*. Athens: Kardamitsas Publications, 1998.

Bury, John Bagnell, and Russell Meiggs. *History of Greece to the Death of Alexander the Great*. London: Macmillan, 1975.

Catalogue of the officially declared archaeological Sites and Monuments of Greece, Prefecture of Attica, vol. XVII, Athens: Ministry of Culture, 2003.

Cawkwell, George. *The Greek Wars: the Failure of Persia*. Oxford: Oxford University Press, 2005.

Connolly, Peter. *I polemiki techni ton archaeon Ellinon, (The Ancient Greek Art of War)*. Athens: Sideris Publications, 1995.

Connolly, Peter. *Greece and Rome at War*. London: Greenhill Books, 1998.

Cook, John Manuel. *The Persian Empire*. London, Melbourne, Toronto: Dent, 1983.

Crete Maritime Museum. Chania: Museum Publications, 1992. (in the Greek language).

Culley, G. R. "The Restoration of Sanctuaries in Attica." I. G., II (2), 1035, *Hesperia* 44 (1975), p. 207 – 223.

Culley, G. R. "The Restoration of Sanctuaries in Attica." II, *Hesperia* 46 (1977), p. 282 – 298.

Diodorus Siculus. *Istoriki vivliothiki*. (Historical library). Athens: Kaktos Publications, 1992.

Diodorus Siculus. *Books 11-12.37.1: Greek History, 480-431 – the Alternative Version*. (Peter Green, translator) Austin: University of Texas Press, 2006.

Garoufalis, D. *Oi Persikoi Polemoi, (The Persian Wars)*. Athens: Periscopio Publications, 2003.

Green, Peter. *Oi ellinopersikoi polemoi, (The Greco-Persian Wars)*. Athens: Tourikis Publications, 2004.

Green, Peter. *The Greco-Persian Wars*. Berkeley: University of California Press, c. 1996.

Hammond, Nicholas G. L. "The Expedition of Xerxes." *Cambridge Ancient History* IV (2), Cambridge: Cambridge University Press, 1988. p. 518 – 591.

Hammond, Nicholas G. L. *Studies in Greek History: a companion volume to A History of Greece to 322 B.C.* Oxford: Clarendon Press, 1973.

Hanson, J. *Oi polemoi ton archaeon Ellinon, (The wars of the ancient Greeks)*. Athens: Enalios Publications, 2005.

Hanson, Victor Davis. *The Wars of the Ancient Greeks: and their invention of western military culture*. London: Cassell, 1999.

Herodotus. *Istoriai, (Histories)*. Athens: Govostis Publications, 1995.

Herodotus. *The Histories*. (Aubrey De Selincourt, translator) London, New York: Penguin, 2003.

Istoria tou Ellinikou Ethnous, (A history of the Greek Nation). Athens: Ekdotiki Athinon Publications, 1977.

Kampouri, M. *I navmachia tis Salaminos, (The naval battle of Salamis)*. Athens: Epikoinonies Publications, 2006.

Kuhrt, Amélie. *The Ancient Near East*. London & New York: Routledge, 1995.

Lazenby, J.F. *Xerxes' Greek adventure: the naval perspective*. Leiden & Boston, 2005.

Mossé, Claude. *Histoire d'une démocratie: Athènes, dès origins à la conquête macédonienne*. [Paris]: Éditions du Seuil, [1971].

Mossé, Claude. *Istoria mias Dimokratias, I Athina apo tin Idrisi tis mechri ti Makedoniki kataktisi, (History of a Democracy: Athens from the beginning to the Macedonian Conquest*. Athens: The National bank of Greece Educational Institute Publications, 1983.

Mossé, Claude, and Annie Schnapp-Gourbeillon. *Istoria tis Archaias Elladas (2000-31 P. Ch.), A History of Ancient Greece (2000-31 B.C.)*. Athens: Papadimas Publications, 1996.

Mossé, Claude and Annie Schnapp-Gourbeillon. *Précis d'histoire Grecque: du début du deuxième millénaire à la bataille d'Actium*. Paris: A. Colin, c. 1990.

Nellopoulos, Emmanouel. *I elliniki triiris, (The Greek trireme)*. Athens: Floros Publications, 199?.

Nellopoulos, Emmanouel. *The Greek Trieres*. (English translation by Philippa Currie). Athens: John Floros Pub. House, 1993?.

Plutarch. *Vioi paralliloi, (Parallel lives)*. Athens: Kaktos Publications, 1991-2.

Plutarch. *The Rise and Fall of Athens: nine Greek lives*. London, New York: Penguin, 1960.

Pritchett, W. Kendrick. "Toward a Restudy of the Battle of Salamis," *American Journal of Archaeology* 63 (1959), p. 251 – 262.

Pritchett, W. Kendrick. *Studies in Ancient Greek Topography*. Berkeley: University of California Press, 1965.

Pritchett, W. Kendrick. *The Greek State at War*. Berkeley: University of California Press, 1985.

Psaroulaki, G. "I navmachia tis Salaminos," ("The naval battle of Salamis"). *Pagkosmia Polemiki Istoria, (World War History)* magazine, 5 (June 2006).

Rados, Konstantinos. *I navmachia tis Salaminos, (The naval battle of Salamis)*. Athens: Enalios Publications, 2004.

Rados, Konstantinos. *La Bataille de Salamine*. Paris: Fontemoing, 1915.

Steinhauer, Georgios. *Oi polemoi stin archaea Ellada, (Warfare in Ancient Greece)*. Athens: Papadimas Publications, 2000.

Tarn, William W. *Stratiotikes kai nautikes ekselikseis kata tin ellinistiki epochi, (Hellenistic military and naval developments)*. Athens: Forminx Publications, 1998.

Tarn, William W. *Hellenistic Military and Naval Developments*. Cambridge: Cambridge University Press, 1930.

Theophrastus. *Enquiry into Plants*. (Arthur F. Hort, translator). Cambridge, Massachusetts: Harvard University Press / Loeb Classical Library, vols, 1, 2, originally published 1916.

Thucydides. *The History of the Peloponnesian War*. (Rex Warner, translator). London, New York: Penguin, 1954.

Tsirivakos, H. "Anaskafes – Magoula", ("Excavations – Magoula"). *Archaeological Bulletin* B1 22 (1967), p. 144 – 146.

Tzachos, E. "I tacheia Triiris," ("The fast trireme"), *Polemos kai Istoria (War and History)* magazine 21. Athens: Epikoinonies Publications, 1999.

Tzachos, E. "I tacheia Triiris – Amyntikes kai epithetikes taktikes," ("The fast trireme – Defensive and offensive tactics"), *Polemos kai Istoria (War and History)* magazine 69, Athens: Epikoinonies Publications, 2003.

Vlachos, Angelos. *Thoukididou Istoria tou Peloponisiakou Polemou, (Thucydides' History of the Peloponnesian War)*. Athens: Estia Bookshop Publications, 1999.

Wallace, Paul W. "Psyttaleia and the Trophies of the Battle of Salamis," *American Journal of Archaeology* 73 (1969), p. 293 – 303.

Wallinga, H. T. *Xerxes' Greek Adventure: the naval Perspective*. Leiden & Boston: Brill, 2005.

Young, T. Cuyler. "480 – 479 B.C. – A Persian Perspective," *Iranica Antiqua* XV (1980), p. 213 – 239.

Young, T. Cuyler. "The Consolidation of the Empire and its Limits of Growth under Darius and Xerxes," *Cambridge Ancient History* IV (2), Cambridge: Cambridge University Press, 1988. pp. 53 – 111.

Young, T. Cuyler. "The Early History of the Medes and the Persians and the Achaemenid Empire to the Death of Cambyses," *Cambridge Ancient History* IV (2), Cambridge: Cambridge University Press, 1988. p. 1 – 52.